THE
SPICY
VEGETARIAN
COOKBOOK

THE
SPICY
VEGETARIAN
COOKBOOK

More Than 200 Fiery Snacks, Dips, & Main Dishes for the Meat-Free Lifestyle

ADAMS MEDIA

Avon, Massachusetts

Published by
Adams Media, a division of F+W Media, Inc.
57 Littlefield Street, Avon, MA 02322 U.S.A.
www.adamsmedia.com

Contains material adapted and abridged from *The Everything® Vegetarian Cookbook* by Jay Weinstein, copyright © 2002 by F+W Media, Inc., ISBN 10: 1-58062-640-8, ISBN 13: 978-1-58062-640-8; *The Everything® Vegetarian Slow Cooker Cookbook* by Amy Snyder and Justin Snyder, copyright © 2012 by F+W Media, Inc., ISBN 10: 1-4405-2858-6, ISBN 13: 978-1-4405-2858-3; *The Everything® Vegetarian Pressure Cooker Cookbook* by Amy Snyder and Justin Snyder, copyright © 2010 by F+W Media, Inc., ISBN 10: 1-4405-0672-8, ISBN 13: 978-1-4405-0672-7; and *The Everything® Hot Sauce Book* by Angela Garbes, copyright © 2012 by F+W Media, Inc., ISBN 10: 1-4405-3011-4, ISBN 13: 978-1-4405-3011-1.

ISBN 10: 1-4405-7326-3
ISBN 13: 978-1-4405-7326-2
epub eISBN 10: 1-4405-7327-1
epub eISBN 13: 978-1-4405-7327-9

Printed in the United States of America.

10 9 8 7 6 5 4 3 2 1

Always follow safety and commonsense cooking protocol while using kitchen utensils, operating ovens and stoves, and handling uncooked food. If children are assisting in the preparation of any recipe, they should always be supervised by an adult.

This book is available at quantity discounts for bulk purchases.
For information, please call 1-800-289-0963.

CONTENTS

Chapter 3: Salads, Hors d'Oeuvres, and Snacks 65

Chapter 4: Salsas and Spice Mixes.. 101

Chapter 5: Soups, Stews, and Chilies 129

Chapter 6: Grains, Beans, and Legumes 151

Chapter 7: Vegetables 171

Chapter 8: Pasta Dishes 199

Chapter 9: Hot and Spicy Desserts and Drinks 209

Appendix A: Metric Conversion Chart 225

Appendix B: Pepper Identification Charts 227

Index 231

INTRODUCTION

Chipotle. Habanero. Jalapeño.

Today, hot and spicy ingredients like these are taking the culinary world by storm and are showing up on the menus of neighborhood diners and fine dining restaurants alike. But finding vegetarian dishes that satisfy your cravings for spice isn't always easy. Fortunately, *The Spicy Vegetarian Cookbook* offers more than two hundred recipes guaranteed to give your palate the heat it's been looking for!

With vegetarian recipes ranging from Poblano Hash Browns to Spicy Mac and Cheese to Red Chili Ice Cream, you'll be able to fire up your table—no matter what meal you're eating! In addition, you'll find recipes like Jalapeño-Tomatillo Sauce, Chipotle Mayo, Mango Habanero Salsa, and Homemade Chili Powder that show you how to make your own sauces, spices, salsas, and spreads so you can take anything on your menu and kick it up a notch.

Throughout the book, you'll find recipes with a variety of spices and levels of heat. Some recipes like Red Pepper Grits show restraint by calling for just a smattering of hot red pepper flakes, while others like the Five-Pepper Chili will have you calling the fire department to put out the heat the spicy habanero pepper left behind.

So whether you're looking for something just a little spicy or out-of-this-world hot, or if you're indulging in an early-morning breakfast or salivating over a late-night dessert, *The Spicy Vegetarian Cookbook* is sure to spice up your life!

CHAPTER 1

Breakfast and Brunch

Spicy Home Fries

Like hash browns, these pressure cooker home fries can also be served with a variety of toppings or with a side of Spicy Ketchup (see Chapter 2).

Serves 4

2 tablespoons olive oil
4 cups red potatoes, diced
1½ teaspoons paprika
1 teaspoon chili powder
1½ teaspoons salt
1 teaspoon black pepper

1. Bring the olive oil to low heat in the pressure cooker. Add the potatoes and sauté for about 3 minutes.

2. Add all remaining ingredients and stir. Lock the lid in place and bring to high pressure; maintain pressure for 7 minutes. Remove from heat and quick-release the pressure.

Scrambled Egg Burritos

This innovative "wrap" adds some spice to breakfast or brunch!

1. In a large skillet over medium heat, melt the butter; add the onion and sliced roasted peppers. Cook until the onion is soft and translucent, about 5 minutes. Combine the eggs and the cream, and add them to the pan. Cook, stirring constantly with a wooden spoon, until the eggs are about half cooked and still very runny; add the hot pepper sauce, cheese, salt, and pepper. Remove from heat. Eggs should be soft, creamy, and have small curds.

2. Soften the tortillas by placing them directly atop the stove burner on medium heat; a few black spots are okay. Spoon ¼ of the egg mixture slightly off center on a tortilla. Fold the sides in upon the egg and roll the tortilla away from yourself, folding the filling in and tucking with your fingers to keep even pressure. Repeat with remaining tortillas. Serve with salsa.

Serves 4

1 tablespoon unsalted butter
1 medium onion, finely chopped
(about 1 cup)
½ cup sliced roasted peppers
9 extra-large eggs, beaten
½ cup half-and-half
Few dashes of hot pepper sauce
2 cups shredded jalapeño jack cheese
Salt and pepper, to taste
4 (12") flour tortillas
Store-bought salsa

Spicy Breakfast Burrito

To make this slow cooker Spicy Breakfast Burrito vegetarian instead of vegan, use cooked eggs instead of tofu.

Serves 4

¼ cup olive oil
1 (16-ounce) package firm tofu, drained and crumbled
¼ cup red onion, diced
1 tablespoon jalapeño, minced
¼ cup red bell pepper, diced
¼ cup poblano pepper, diced
1 cup cooked black beans, drained
2 teaspoons turmeric
1 teaspoon cumin
½ teaspoon chili powder
1 teaspoon salt
¼ teaspoon black pepper
4 large flour tortillas
1 avocado, peeled and sliced
½ cup tomato, diced
¼ cup cilantro, chopped
½ cup chipotle salsa
½ cup shredded Cheddar cheese or vegan Cheddar cheese

1. Add olive oil, tofu, onion, jalapeño, red bell pepper, and poblano pepper to a 4-quart slow cooker and sauté on medium-high for 5–8 minutes.

2. Add the black beans, turmeric, cumin, chili powder, salt, and black pepper. Cover and cook on high heat for 4 hours.

3. Scoop the filling onto the tortillas and add the avocado, tomato, cilantro, salsa, and cheese. Fold the sides of the tortilla in and roll up the burrito.

🌶 STEAMING TORTILLAS

For best results, steam tortillas on the stovetop using a steamer basket. If you're in a hurry, throw the tortillas into the microwave one at a time and heat for about 30 seconds.

Red Pepper Grits

Cooking these hot and spicy Red Pepper Grits using Vegetable Stock in the pressure cooker adds more depth to the flavor and makes them more appropriate for dinner or lunch.

1. Bring the Vegetable Stock, salt, and thyme to a boil in the pressure cooker over high heat. Slowly stir in the grits.

2. Lock the lid into place. Bring to high pressure and maintain for 10 minutes. Remove from heat and allow pressure to release naturally.

3. Remove the lid and stir in the red pepper flakes before serving.

Serves 4

4 cups Vegetable Stock (see Chapter 5)
1 teaspoon salt
¼ teaspoon dried thyme
1 cup stone-ground grits
½ tablespoon dried red pepper flakes

♨ GRITS

Grits are a southern breakfast staple that are served topped with butter or margarine, salt, pepper, and sometimes cheese. They're very similar to polenta, especially when polenta is served creamy.

Onion, Pepper, and Potato Hash Browns

Use a cheese grater to grate the potatoes for this spicy slow cooker dish.

Serves 4

2 tablespoons olive oil
4 cups russet potatoes, peeled and grated
½ onion, diced
1 poblano pepper, cored and diced
2 cloves garlic, minced
1 teaspoon chili powder
½ teaspoon paprika
½ teaspoon cumin
1 teaspoon salt
¼ teaspoon pepper

Add all ingredients to a 4-quart slow cooker. Cover and cook on high heat for 4 hours.

Poblano Hash Browns

Any type of pepper will do, such as poblano, jalapeño, or bell pepper, in these spicy, pressure cooker Poblano Hash Browns.

1. Prepare the grated potatoes by rinsing in a colander, then air-drying or using a towel to remove excess water.

2. Add the oil and butter or margarine to the pressure cooker and bring to temperature over high heat. Add the onion and poblano pepper and sauté until just soft, about 5 minutes.

3. Add the garlic and potatoes; sauté for an additional 5 minutes, stirring occasionally, until they are just beginning to brown. Season with the salt, pepper, and cumin.

4. Use a wide metal spatula to press the potatoes down firmly in the pan.

5. Lock the lid in place and bring to low pressure; maintain pressure for 6 minutes. Remove from heat and quick-release the pressure.

Serves 4

4 cups russet potatoes, peeled and grated
2 tablespoons olive oil
2 tablespoons butter or vegan margarine, such as Earth Balance
¼ cup onion, diced
1 poblano pepper, cored and diced
1 clove garlic, minced
Salt and freshly ground pepper, to taste
1 teaspoon cumin

Jalapeño Hash Browns

The type of jalapeños you choose for this dish can make the heat vary greatly, so be careful if you don't like it hot.

Serves 6

2 tablespoons olive oil
2 pounds red potatoes, peeled and shredded
1 onion, diced
¼ cup pickled jalapeños, chopped
1 teaspoon salt
¼ teaspoon black pepper

Place all ingredients in a 4-quart slow cooker, cover, and cook on high 2 hours.

Spicy Three-Pepper Frittata

Frittatas are traditionally made with eggs, but you can use tofu to make this easy, pressure cooker Spicy Three-Pepper Frittata cholesterol free instead.

1. Preheat the oven to 400°F.

2. Bring the olive oil to low heat in the pressure cooker. Add the potatoes, onion, peppers, garlic, and parsley, and sauté for 3 minutes. Lock the lid in place and bring to high pressure; maintain pressure for 6 minutes. Remove from heat and quick-release the pressure.

3. Combine the tofu, soymilk, cornstarch, nutritional yeast, mustard, turmeric, and salt in a blender or food processor until smooth, then pour the tofu mixture into the cooked potato mixture.

4. Spoon the mixture into an oiled quiche or pie pan. Bake for 45 minutes, or until the frittata is firm, then remove from heat and let stand before serving.

Serves 4

2 tablespoons olive oil
1 cup red potatoes, peeled and diced
½ cup onion, diced
½ cup red bell pepper, diced
½ cup green bell pepper, diced
1 teaspoon jalapeño, minced
1 clove garlic, minced
¼ cup chopped parsley
1 (16-ounce) package firm tofu
½ cup unsweetened soymilk
4 teaspoons cornstarch
2 teaspoons nutritional yeast
1 teaspoon mustard
½ teaspoon turmeric
1 teaspoon salt

🌶 MAKE IT A SCRAMBLE

To shorten the preparation time for this meal while keeping all of the flavors, try making this dish into a scramble by preparing the entire recipe in the pressure cooker. Skip the step of blending the tofu and omit the cornstarch. Add remaining ingredients, breaking apart tofu as you stir, and sauté until cooked through.

Chinese Soy Sauce Eggs

These spicy, strikingly dark, double-cooked spiced eggs are an excellent first course with a salad of baby Asian greens dressed with a few drops of rice vinegar and sesame oil.

Serves 4

8 large eggs
4 cups water
½ cup soy sauce
2 tablespoons sugar
2 tablespoons Chinese 5-spice powder (available in super-markets)
1 tablespoon chopped garlic

Hard-boil the eggs, about 10 minutes; run them under cold water, and peel them. Bring 4 cups water to a boil in a medium sauce-pan. Add the soy sauce and sugar. Simmer 5 minutes; add the 5-spice powder, garlic, and peeled eggs. Cover; simmer slowly for at least an hour, until the soy sauce's color has penetrated well into the eggs, all the way to the yolk. Cool in the cooking liquid, and serve warm or at room temperature.

Spicy Slow Cooker Tofu Scramble

Serve this spicy scramble on its own or rolled up in a flour tortilla to make a delicious breakfast burrito.

1. Add the oil to a 4-quart slow cooker and sauté the onion, red pepper, and garlic on low heat for about 3 minutes.

2. Mix in the tofu, turmeric, cumin, chipotle powder, chili powder, salt, and black pepper. Cover and cook on high heat for 2–4 hours.

3. About 5 minutes before the scramble is finished, add the tomato, lemon juice, and cilantro.

Serves 4

2 tablespoons olive oil
½ onion, diced
½ red pepper, diced
2 cloves garlic, minced
1 (16-ounce) package firm tofu, drained and crumbled
2 teaspoons turmeric
1 teaspoon cumin
½ teaspoon chipotle powder
½ teaspoon chili powder
1 teaspoon salt
¼ teaspoon black pepper
¼ cup tomato, diced
1 lemon, juiced
2 tablespoons fresh cilantro, chopped

Tofu Ranchero

Bring Mexican cuisine to the breakfast table with this easy Tofu Ranchero cooked in your slow cooker.

Serves 4

3 tablespoons olive oil

1 (16-ounce) package firm tofu, drained and crumbled

½ onion, diced

2 cloves garlic, minced

1 lemon, juiced

½ teaspoon turmeric

1 teaspoon salt

¼ teaspoon black pepper

1 cup cooked pinto beans, drained

8 corn tortillas

½ cup shredded Cheddar cheese or vegan Cheddar cheese

½ cup chipotle salsa

1. Add the olive oil, tofu, onion, garlic, lemon, turmeric, salt, black pepper, and pinto beans to a 4-quart slow cooker. Cover and cook on high heat for 4 hours.

2. When the ranchero filling is nearly done, brown the tortillas on both sides using a small sauté pan.

3. Preheat the oven to 350°F.

4. Place the tortillas on a baking sheet and add the filling. Sprinkle the cheese over the rancheros and bake until the cheese has melted, about 5 minutes. Top with the chipotle salsa.

Huevos Rancheros

Rich and delicious, this Mexican ranch breakfast will fuel your whole morning, even if you're climbing Mt. Everest that day. While this recipe calls for scrambled eggs, it works equally well with any style of eggs.

1. Heat the beans and Rancheros Salsa in separate pots over low flames. Scramble together the eggs, half-and-half, and salt. Melt the butter in a nonstick pan; cook the scrambled eggs over a low flame until soft and creamy, with small curds.

2. Soften the tortillas either by steaming or flash-cooking over an open gas burner. Place 2 tortillas onto each plate. Divide the hot black beans evenly onto these tortillas. Spoon the eggs onto the beans, then sauce with a ladleful of Rancheros Salsa. Garnish with cheese, sour cream, and cilantro. Serve immediately.

Serves 4

1 can Mexican-style black beans in sauce
2 cups Rancheros Salsa (see Chapter 4) or store-bought Mexican salsa
8 large eggs
½ cup half-and-half
½ teaspoon salt
2 tablespoons unsalted butter
8 soft corn tortillas (8" diameter)
1 cup shredded Monterey jack or mild Cheddar cheese
½ cup sour cream
Chopped cilantro

Foul

Foul (pronounced "FOOL") is a classic Egyptian breakfast. A far cry from sugary sweet cereal, it's spicy and satisfying and tastes best when scooped with pieces of warm pita or crusty French bread.

Serves 4

2 tablespoons olive oil
2 garlic cloves, peeled and finely
  chopped
1 small onion, finely chopped
1 large tomato, seeded and
  roughly chopped, separated
  into 2 equal portions
½ teaspoon chili powder
½ teaspoon ground cumin
1 (19-ounce) can of fava beans,
  with liquid
1 small cucumber, peeled,
  seeded, and finely chopped
2 jalapeño peppers, seeded and
  finely chopped
Handful of fresh parsley and
  mint leaves, finely chopped
Juice of half a lemon
½ cup olive oil

1. Heat olive oil in the bottom of a saucepan. Add garlic, onion, half the tomato, chili powder, and cumin. Sauté until soft and fragrant, about 3–4 minutes.

2. Add the fava beans and liquid. Bring to a boil, then lower heat and let simmer for 10–15 minutes. Remove from heat and let cool. Drain beans and reserve the liquid.

3. Put beans in a large bowl and toss with cucumber, jalapeño peppers, herbs, lemon juice, and olive oil. If you like a little more sauce, add a little of the reserved cooking liquid.

4. Serve in bowls with pita or French bread.

🔥 FAVA BEANS

Fava beans are native to North Africa and used extensively in North African and Middle Eastern cooking. Fava beans are a key ingredient in staple dishes like falafel, soups, and stews. If you can't find fava beans at the store, you can substitute canned or dried brown beans.

Chilaquiles

Chilaquiles are a great, easy way to use up extra salsa and tortillas you might have around the house. Add a couple of fried eggs on top for a savory breakfast.

1. Heat the oil in skillet. Add the tortilla pieces and fry until they start to turn light brown. Add the onion and salt and keep frying 3–4 minutes longer, until the onion is soft and beginning to brown.

2. Turn the heat down and add the salsa. Stir well so that all the tortillas soak up some of the salsa. Continue cooking until salsa is heated through, about 1–2 minutes.

3. Transfer chilaquiles to a plate and top with cheese and toppings of your choice.

Serves 4

2 tablespoons vegetable oil
8 corn tortillas, each cut into 8 triangles
½ onion, roughly chopped
Salt, to taste
½–1 cup of your favorite salsa
Handful of crumbled queso fresco or Cotija cheese

🔥 CHILAQUILES

The term chilaquiles translates to "broken up old sombrero," but in actuality it's a way of using up old, stale tortillas. Nearly every region in Mexico has its own version of chilaquiles, some with meat, some with creamy cheese toppings. Pretty much anything goes with this dish, so long as you start with tortillas and salsa. Use up leftovers from your refrigerator—you really can't go wrong.

Tofu Frittata

Frittata is an Italian word that derives from "to fry." Let this fiery dish spice up your morning!

Serves 4

2 tablespoons olive oil
1 cup red potatoes, peeled and diced
½ onion, diced
½ cup red pepper, diced
½ cup green pepper, diced
1 teaspoon jalapeño, minced
1 clove garlic, minced
¼ cup parsley
1 (16-ounce) package firm tofu
½ cup unsweetened soymilk
4 teaspoons cornstarch
2 tablespoons nutritional yeast
1 teaspoon mustard
½ teaspoon turmeric
1 teaspoon salt
¼ teaspoon black pepper

1. Add the oil to a large pan and sauté the potatoes, onion, peppers, jalapeño, and garlic on medium heat for about 15–20 minutes.

2. Meanwhile, in a blender or food processor, combine the rest of the ingredients until smooth, then pour the mixture into the slow cooker with the potatoes.

3. Cover and cook on high heat for 4 hours, or until the frittata has firmed.

CHAPTER 2

Sauces and Spreads

SAUCES

Chinese Chili Oil

Harissa

Zhug

Tequila Hot Sauce

Jalapeño-Tomatillo Sauce

Puttanesca Sauce

Kansas City–Style Barbecue Sauce

Texas-Style Barbecue Sauce

Spicy Ketchup

New Mexico Chili Sauce

Mole

Coconut Curry Sauce

Slow Cooker Three-Pepper Sauce

Pressure Cooker Roasted Red Pepper
  Sauce

Piri Piri Sauce

Green Curry Paste

Red Curry Paste

Sakay

Sambal

Homemade Sriracha

Chermoula

Chimichurri

Indonesian Peanut Sauce

Chipotle Hollandaise Sauce

Romesco Sauce

Jerk Sauce

SPREADS

Ajvar

Red Garlic Mayonnaise

Chipotle Mayo

Chili-Orange Butter for Grilled Bread

Fresh Tomato Chutney

Green Tomato Chutney

Green Coriander Chutney

Mango Chutney

Caribbean Relish

Chinese Chili Oil

This easy-to-assemble chili oil is a great hot sauce to have on hand in your kitchen. Drizzle it into stir fries, rice, and soup. When you use it, make sure to scoop some of those flavorful bits that settle on the bottom.

Yields about 3 cups

⅔ cup dried red chili flakes
⅓ cup Chinese fermented black beans, roughly chopped
4 large cloves garlic, peeled and lightly smashed
2 tablespoons fresh ginger, peeled and finely minced
2½ cups peanut oil
⅓ cup sesame oil

1. Combine all ingredients in a heavy, non-aluminum saucepan. Rest a thermometer on the rim of the pot. Bring the mixture to a bubble over low-to-medium heat (between 225°F–250°F), stirring occasionally. Let it simmer 15 minutes, making sure the temperature doesn't rise.

2. Remove from the heat and let stand until cool.

3. Pour the oil and solids into a clean glass jar. Cover and store in the refrigerator. Take it out of the fridge and let it come to room temperature before using.

🔥 WHAT ARE CHINESE BLACK BEANS?

Chinese black beans are nothing like the black beans you'll find in burritos or Mexican restaurants. These fermented black beans (also called salted or dried black beans) are actually soybeans that have been dried and fermented with salt. They have a pungent, salty flavor and are used throughout Chinese cooking.

Harissa

Harissa is a Tunisian hot sauce that is used throughout North African cooking. Extra spices give it a great flavor that is much more than simply spicy. Harissa adds a welcome boost to cooked lentils, beans, and soups.

1. Soak the chili peppers in hot water for 15 minutes, or until they are nice and soft.

2. Drain the peppers, then combine with garlic, spices, and salt in a food processor.

3. Blend the ingredients, adding a little bit of olive oil, to make a paste.

4. Pour into a clean glass jar and cover with a little oil. Refrigerated, it will keep for a few weeks.

Yields ¼ cup

2 ounces (about 15–20) dried hot red chili peppers, stems and seeds removed
4 cloves garlic, peeled
1 teaspoon ground caraway
1 teaspoon ground coriander
½ teaspoon salt
2–4 tablespoons olive oil

🔥 GRINDING SPICES

You can buy ground spices at the supermarket, but consider buying them whole and grinding them as needed. It only takes a few seconds to grind them (you can use an electric coffee grinder or do it by hand with a mortar and pestle) and you'll notice that the flavors are stronger and brighter.

Zhug

Zhug is a downright fiery sauce that is eaten daily in Yemen, where it's believed to keep away illness. One taste of its potent garlic flavor and you'll understand why. A little zhug goes a long way on sandwiches.

Yields about 1 cup

1 bunch of cilantro, stems included

3–6 serrano peppers, depending on your preference, seeded (if you like it very spicy, feel free to leave the ribs and seeds in)

6 garlic cloves, peeled and roughly chopped (resist the urge to use less)

½ teaspoon ground cumin

Salt, to taste

Olive oil

Lemon juice, to taste

1. Wash the cilantro well and pat dry. Coarsely chop leaves and stems. Place in a food processor.

2. Add the chopped serranos, garlic, cumin, and salt to the food processor.

3. Blend. Add enough olive oil to make a rough paste.

4. Taste and adjust seasoning to your liking. Add lemon juice, to taste.

5. Place in a clean jar. Refrigerated, this will keep for a few weeks.

Tequila Hot Sauce

This simple, boozy sauce will become more flavorful the longer it sits. Also, the higher quality the tequila you use, the better the sauce will be.

1. Toast allspice, peppercorns, and cumin in a skillet over medium heat until they are fragrant, about 2–3 minutes. Remove from heat and set aside.

2. Unscrew the tequila bottle and take a shot or two (or just pour out about 1" worth from the bottle) to make room for other ingredients.

3. Add the spices and chilies to the tequila bottle.

4. Screw the top back on (or add a pour spout). Let sauce sit for 1 week before using.

Yields 1 pint

¼ teaspoon whole allspice
¼ teaspoon black peppercorns
¼ teaspoon cumin seeds
1 pint tequila blanco
5 fresh red Thai chilies, lightly smashed with the side of a knife (you could also use dried chilies)

🔥 DIFFERENT TYPES OF TEQUILA

Tequila blanco, or "white tequila," is unaged and bottled immediately after distillation. It tastes cleaner and a bit harsher than other types of tequilas. Tequila reposado ("rested") is aged in oak barrels for at least two months, while añejo ("aged") stays in oak barrels for at least one year. These tequilas are smoother and more complex tasting.

Jalapeño-Tomatillo Sauce

Serve this spicy sauce over rice or in burritos or tacos.

Serves 4

1 teaspoon canola oil
2 cloves garlic, minced
1 onion, sliced
7 tomatillos, diced
2 jalapeños, minced
½ cup water

1. In a nonstick pan, heat the oil. Add the garlic, onion, tomatillos, and jalapeños and sauté about 5 minutes.

2. In a 4-quart slow cooker, place the mixture; add the water and stir. Cover and cook on low for 8 hours.

Puttanesca Sauce

The crushed red pepper adds a substantial kick to this spicy, slow cooker dish!

1. In a large sauté pan, heat the olive oil over medium heat. Add the garlic and onion and sauté until soft, about 3–4 minutes.

2. In a 4-quart slow cooker, place the onion and garlic; add the remaining ingredients. Stir to distribute the ingredients evenly.

3. Cook on low for 4–6 hours. If the sauce looks very wet at the end of the cooking time, remove the lid and cook on high for 15–30 minutes before serving.

Serves 6

1 tablespoon olive oil
4 cloves garlic, minced
1 onion, diced
1 cup sliced black olives
1 tablespoon olive brine
1 (28-ounce) can crushed tomatoes
1 (15-ounce) can diced tomatoes
3 tablespoons crushed red pepper
2 tablespoons drained nonpareil-size capers
2 tablespoons fresh basil, chopped

🔥 WHAT IS SAUTÉING?

Sautéing is a method of cooking that uses a small amount of fat to cook food in a shallow pan over medium-high heat. The goal is to brown the food while preserving its color, moisture, and flavor.

Kansas City–Style Barbecue Sauce

This is a classic, all-purpose barbecue sauce to use on all kinds of dishes. Slather this onto grilled foods or use it as a dipping sauce on your plate. For extra spice, add more cayenne.

Yields about 2 cups

3 tablespoons vegetable oil
1 medium onion, finely minced
½ cup celery, finely chopped
4 garlic cloves, peeled and minced
¾ cup apple cider vinegar
½ cup tomato paste
½ cup water
2 tablespoons molasses
3 tablespoons light brown sugar
2 tablespoons vegan Worcestershire sauce
2 teaspoons hot paprika
1 teaspoon powdered mustard
½ teaspoon ground black pepper
½ teaspoon cayenne pepper
1 tablespoon kosher salt

1. In a heavy saucepan, heat the vegetable oil over medium heat. Add the onion, celery, and garlic, and cook until softened, about 5 minutes.

2. Add the rest of the ingredients and simmer the sauce, uncovered, for 30 minutes, stirring occasionally. The sauce should be quite thick.

3. Purée the sauce in a blender until smooth.

4. Store in an airtight container in the refrigerator, where it will keep for a couple of weeks.

Texas-Style Barbecue Sauce

This barbecue sauce is thinner and less sweet than the Kansas City–Style Barbecue Sauce, but it's also got the added bonus of the flavor and spices of the Southwest. Feel free to turn up the heat with a little extra chili powder.

1. In a heavy saucepan, heat the vegetable oil over medium heat. Add the onions, celery, and garlic, and cook until softened, about 5 minutes.

2. Add all the remaining ingredients and simmer the sauce, uncovered and stirring occasionally, for 20 minutes. It should be quite thick.

3. Purée the sauce in a blender until smooth.

4. Store in an airtight container in the refrigerator, where it will keep for a couple of weeks.

Yields about 3 cups

¼ cup vegetable oil
2 large onions, minced
¼ cup celery, finely chopped
4 garlic cloves, peeled and minced
½ cup apple cider vinegar
¼ cup distilled white vinegar
¾ cup ketchup
½ cup tomato sauce
½ cup water
2 tablespoons vegan Worcestershire sauce
1 tablespoon chili powder
1½ teaspoons ground cumin
1 teaspoon hot paprika
1 tablespoon coarse salt

♨ DIFFERENT STYLES OF BARBECUE

Barbecue is a highly contentious matter for many Americans, especially in the South. What Texans think of as barbecue is nothing like what people from North Carolina picture (to say nothing of the difference between western and eastern Carolina barbecue). Carolina sauces are generally more vinegary than Texas and Kansas City sauces. One thing everyone agrees on: Whatever the style, barbecue sauce makes everything even more delicious.

Spicy Ketchup

It may seem crazy at first to make your own ketchup, but homemade ketchup is much better tasting and far less sweet than the bottled stuff. (It's also better for you because it's not loaded with high fructose corn syrup.) Think ketchup, but with a spicy twist. Use it on the usual suspects—burgers, french fries, and eggs.

Yields about 2 cups

1 (28-ounce) can whole tomatoes
2 tablespoons olive oil
1 medium onion, finely chopped
1 tablespoon tomato paste
⅓ cup packed dark brown sugar
¼ cup apple cider vinegar
½ teaspoon salt
½ teaspoon crushed red pepper flakes
¼ teaspoon ground cayenne pepper
½ teaspoon ground cumin

1. Purée the canned whole tomatoes (along with their juices) in a blender until smooth.

2. In a heavy saucepan heat the oil over medium heat and cook the onion until softened, about 5 minutes.

3. Add the puréed tomatoes and rest of the ingredients and simmer, uncovered and stirring occasionally, until the mixture is quite thick, about an hour.

4. Purée the ketchup in batches in a blender until smooth. Cover the top of the blender with a towel and be careful when blending hot liquids, as they will expand.

5. Transfer the ketchup to a clean, airtight container. Let chill for at least 2 hours before using. Store in the refrigerator.

New Mexico Chili Sauce

This tomato-based southwestern sauce is the ultimate salsa for Scrambled Egg Burritos (see Chapter 1), a wonderful accompaniment to scrambled eggs or omelets, and the base for the sauce in Chilaquiles (see Chapter 1).

Heat the oil in a saucepan over a medium flame. Add onion; cook, stirring occasionally, until translucent, about 5 minutes. Add chili purée; cook 3 minutes more. Add the marinara sauce, cumin, and oregano. Simmer 10 minutes. Purée in a blender until very smooth.

Yields 3 cups

1 teaspoon olive oil
1 medium onion, roughly chopped
5 New Mexico chilies, seeded, soaked, and puréed
1 (28-ounce) jar roasted-garlic-flavored marinara sauce
½ teaspoon ground cumin
½ teaspoon dried oregano

Mole

Just like barbecue sauce in the United States, mole sauce recipes vary greatly by region, and no two are exactly the same. But whatever your preference, this spicy, slow cooker Mole sauce is sure to spice up your day!

Yields 2 cups

2 tablespoons olive oil
½ onion, finely diced
3 garlic cloves, minced
1 teaspoon ground cumin
¼ teaspoon ground cinnamon
¼ teaspoon ground coriander
1 tablespoon chili powder
2 chipotle peppers in adobo, seeded and minced
1 teaspoon salt
4 cups Vegetable Stock (see Chapter 5)
1 ounce vegan dark chocolate, chopped

1. In a sauté pan over medium heat, add the oil, onion, and garlic and sauté about 3 minutes. Add the cumin, cinnamon, and coriander and sauté for 1 minute.

2. Transfer the sautéed mixture to a 4-quart slow cooker. Add the chili powder, chipotles, and salt, then whisk in the Vegetable Stock. Finally, add the chocolate.

3. Cover and cook over high heat for 2 hours.

Coconut Curry Sauce

Red curry paste is ideal for this slow cooker recipe, but any variety will do.

1. In a 4-quart slow cooker, add all ingredients except cilantro. Cover and cook on low heat for 2 hours.

2. Add the chopped cilantro and cook for an additional 30 minutes.

Yields about 2 cups

1 (14-ounce) can coconut milk
1 cup Vegetable Stock (see Chapter 5)
1 teaspoon soy sauce
1 tablespoon curry paste
1 tablespoon lime juice
2 cloves garlic, minced
½ teaspoon salt
¼ cup chopped cilantro

Slow Cooker Three-Pepper Sauce

Spicy cayenne peppers are most commonly found dried and ground in the herbs and spices aisle of your grocery store.

Serves 4

1 (28-ounce) can diced tomatoes
2 tablespoons tomato paste
1 red bell pepper, finely diced
1 green bell pepper, finely diced
½ red onion, diced
3 cloves garlic, minced
1 teaspoon cayenne pepper
½ teaspoon sugar
½ teaspoon salt

In a 4-quart slow cooker, add all ingredients. Cover and cook on low heat for 6–8 hours.

Pressure Cooker Roasted Red Pepper Sauce

Save time by using canned or jarred roasted red peppers instead of roasting them yourself. The peppers' spiciness won't be affected and you'll have more time to enjoy!

1. Purée the red peppers, Vegetable Stock, vinegar, and oil in a food processor or blender. Pour the mixture into the pressure cooker and add the garlic powder.

2. Lock the lid into place and bring to high pressure. Once the pressure is achieved, turn the heat to low and cook for about 5 minutes. Remove from heat and allow pressure to release naturally.

3. Add the basil and season with salt and pepper, to taste, before serving.

Serves 4

2 cups roasted red peppers
2 cups Vegetable Stock (see Chapter 5)
2 tablespoons red wine vinegar
2 tablespoons extra-virgin olive oil
1 teaspoon garlic powder
½ cup chopped fresh basil
Salt and pepper, to taste

Piri Piri Sauce

Piri piri is the Swahili term for hot chili. It's also the name of Mozambique's national dish.

Yields about 1 cup

8–10 red bird's eye chilies, seeds and ribs removed, chopped
6 tablespoons fresh lime juice
4 teaspoons dark brown sugar
1 tablespoon olive oil
1 tablespoon fresh ginger, finely chopped
½ tablespoon white vinegar
½ teaspoon kosher salt
2 cloves garlic, peeled and roughly chopped

1. In a blender, combine all the ingredients and purée into a chunky sauce.

2. Transfer to a clean jar and store in the refrigerator for up to 1 week.

Green Curry Paste

Sure, you can buy green curry paste, but making it from scratch is not only easy, it will make your kitchen smell incredible. You'll probably need to open a can of coconut milk to make this, so use the rest of its contents to make a curry for dinner.

1. Place all the ingredients in a food processor or blender.

2. Purée into a smooth paste, adding a little more coconut milk if necessary.

3. Taste and adjust seasoning. If it's too salty, add more lime juice. Add extra chili for more spice.

4. Place in an airtight container. In the refrigerator, it will keep for about 1 week.

Yields 1 cup

1 stalk lemongrass, outer leaves removed and discarded, inner core finely chopped
2 green chilies (you can use Thai chilies or jalapeños), roughly chopped
1 shallot, roughly chopped
4 cloves of garlic, peeled and roughly chopped
1 thumb-size piece of ginger, peeled and thinly sliced
1 bunch cilantro, stems included, roughly chopped
½ cup fresh basil
½ teaspoon ground cumin
3 tablespoons vegetarian "fish" sauce
2 tablespoons lime juice
1 teaspoon brown sugar
3 tablespoons coconut milk, or enough to help blend ingredients together and make paste

Red Curry Paste

Some folks prefer the tartness of green curry, others the pungency of red.

Yields about ½ cup

3 tablespoons coriander seeds, toasted

2 teaspoons cumin seeds, toasted

6–8 red serrano chilies, seeded and chopped

1 medium onion, chopped

2 garlic cloves, chopped

1 stalk lemongrass, outer leaves removed and discarded, inner core finely chopped

1 thumb-size piece of ginger, finely chopped

2 tablespoons lime juice

2 teaspoons hot paprika

2 tablespoons tamarind concentrate

3 tablespoons vegetarian "fish" sauce

3 tablespoons coconut milk, or enough to make a paste

1. Place all the ingredients in a food processor or blender.

2. Purée into a smooth paste, adding a little more coconut milk if necessary.

3. Taste and adjust seasoning. If it's too salty, add more lime juice. Add extra chili for more spice.

4. Place in an airtight container. In the refrigerator, it will keep for about 1 week.

Sakay

Sakay is the everyday hot sauce of choice in the African island nation of Madagascar. The flavors represent the country's long history of African, Arab, and Indonesian settlers. Try this on sandwiches.

1. In a sauté pan over medium heat, toast the chili powder, ginger, cayenne, cumin, and garlic until they are nice and fragrant, about 1–2 minutes. Remove from heat and let cool.

2. Put the spice mix in a food processor, add the salt, and blend well. While the blender is still running, slowly pour the oil in a steady stream until a paste is formed.

3. Store in an airtight container in the refrigerator for up to 2 weeks.

Yields about 1 cup

¾ cup chili powder
1 tablespoon ground ginger
1 teaspoon cayenne pepper
1 teaspoon ground cumin
4 garlic cloves, peeled and minced
2 teaspoons salt
1 cup peanut or vegetable oil

Sambal

In Malaysia and Indonesia, sambal is essential to cooking. There are endless sambal variations; it is the cornerstone of many dishes. This basic but very pungent sambal recipe is wonderful on rice.

Yields about ½ cup

1 tablespoon vegan shrimp paste (available online)
½ cup red jalapeño or Fresno chilies, seeded and thinly sliced
1 teaspoon sugar
2 tablespoons fresh lime juice
Salt, to taste

1. In a saucepan over medium heat, heat the shrimp paste until it dries slightly, about 2 minutes. Make sure to turn the stove fan on, as this will produce a strong scent. Remove from heat and let cool.

2. Put the rest of the ingredients into a food processor. Add the shrimp paste, then blend into a smooth paste.

3. Transfer to an airtight container and keep in the refrigerator for up to 1 week.

Homemade Sriracha

Everybody knows sriracha, a.k.a. "rooster sauce," so named for the most well-known brand, which comes in the clear plastic bottle with a rooster on it and a bright green cap. Chefs and home cooks alike use sriracha in a wide range of dishes. True sriracha fans might want to take the next step and try making it at home with this quick recipe. Feel free to adjust the garlic or sugar to your liking.

1. Put the peppers, garlic, salt, sugar, vinegar, and water in a small saucepan. Bring to a boil, then lower heat and let simmer for 5 minutes. Remove from heat and let cool to room temperature.

2. Purée the mixture in a blender for about 5 minutes, adding water if necessary, until the sauce is smooth.

3. Strain the sauce into a clean bowl. Taste and adjust seasoning.

4. Transfer sauce to a jar and let sit for a few hours so the flavors can come together. Store in the refrigerator, where it will keep for about 1 month.

Yields about 1½ cups

¾ pound fresh red peppers such as Fresno, Holland, or cayenne, seeded and roughly chopped

4 cloves of garlic, peeled and roughly chopped

1¼ teaspoons kosher salt

2 tablespoons palm sugar (available at Asian markets), or 2 tablespoons light brown sugar

¼ cup white vinegar

½ cup water

Chermoula

Chermoula is a hot sauce used all over northern Africa. It has a wonderful citrus flavor and is also nice on grilled veggies.

Yields 1½ cups

8 garlic cloves, peeled and roughly chopped
½ cup parsley leaves and stems, roughly chopped
⅓ cup cilantro leaves and stems, roughly chopped
Grated zest of 2 lemons
4 teaspoons hot paprika
2 teaspoons chili powder
2 teaspoons ground cumin
1 cup olive oil

1. Combine all the ingredients except for oil in a blender. Purée on low until it forms a course paste.

2. With the blender running, slowly add oil in a steady stream until a smooth, thick paste forms.

3. Store in an airtight container in the refrigerator for up to 2 weeks.

Chimichurri

A staple in Argentina, chimichurri is a quick and easy way to use up a lot of parsley. It gets heat from a little bit of red pepper flakes, but feel free to add more. Chimichurri is magnificent when tossed with pasta.

1. Place all the ingredients in a blender or food processor and purée until it forms a coarsely ground paste.

2. Serve immediately or store in an air-tight container in the refrigerator for up to 1 month. If the oil solidifies, bring it to room temperature before use.

🔥 THE LEGEND OF CHIMICHURRI

The exact origin of chimichurri is unknown, but one popular legend is that it is named after an Irishman, Jimmy McCurry, an Argentinian sympathizer who helped fight for the country's independence in the nineteenth century. Supposedly he was the first person to make this sauce, which became wildly popular. Unfortunately, the name Jimmy McCurry was hard for natives to pronounce, resulting in the word chimichurri.

Yields about 1 cup

1 bunch of flat-leaf parsley, roughly chopped

4 garlic cloves, peeled and roughly chopped

2 tablespoons fresh oregano, roughly chopped (you could also use dried oregano, in which case 1 teaspoon will be plenty)

½ cup olive oil

2 tablespoons red wine vinegar

½ teaspoon red pepper flakes

Salt and pepper, to taste

Indonesian Peanut Sauce

This is the sauce to serve with satay for dipping. It's spicy. It's delicious. What more can you ask for?

Yields 1 cup

½ cup smooth peanut butter
½ cup water
1 tablespoon minced red chili pepper (jalapeño or serrano)
2 garlic cloves, minced
2 teaspoons brown sugar
1 teaspoon grated fresh ginger
2 teaspoons lemon juice
1 tablespoon soy sauce
1 tablespoon chopped peanuts

1. Heat the peanut butter and water in a saucepan over low heat, whisking to smooth out the peanut butter.

2. Add the chili pepper, garlic, brown sugar, ginger, and lemon juice and continue to cook over low heat for a few minutes, stirring to prevent scorching.

3. Stir in the soy sauce and remove from heat.

4. Stir in the chopped peanuts.

5. Serve with a variety of things such as skewered veggies or tofu.

Chipotle Hollandaise Sauce

Put this sauce in a thermos to keep it warm while you prepare the food it will be served with. Spicy eggs Benedict, anyone?

1. Whisk egg yolks and water in a stainless steel or glass bowl over simmering water and cook until mixture thickens. Be careful not to overcook or scramble the yolks.

2. Slowly pour the melted butter into the yolks, drop by drop at first, whisking constantly to form an emulsion. Pour the butter in a thin stream after the emulsion gets started and the sauce starts to thicken; continue whisking.

3. Remove bowl from heat and whisk in the lemon juice and chipotle pepper purée.

4. Season sauce with salt and white pepper, to taste.

Yields 1½ cups

4 egg yolks
1 tablespoon cold water
8 ounces butter, melted
1 tablespoon lemon juice
2 cans chipotle peppers, puréed
Salt, to taste
White pepper, to taste

Romesco Sauce

Romesco is a classic Spanish sauce that originates in Catalonia. Traditionally it's made with the nyora peppers grown in the region, though here you can substitute roasted red peppers.

Yields 1–2 cups

3 large plum tomatoes
2 large red bell peppers
1 medium onion, halved
¼ cup olive oil, plus more for roasting and sautéing
1 dried ancho chili, plus boiling water to cover
½ cup sliced almonds
3 garlic cloves, peeled and smashed
2 tablespoons sherry vinegar
1 slice toasted white bread (or day-old bread), cut into cubes
1 tablespoon Spanish smoked paprika
¼ teaspoon cayenne pepper
Salt and pepper, to taste

1. Heat oven to 400°F. Put tomatoes, bell peppers, and onion in a baking dish and drizzle with olive oil. Roast until charred and soft, turning once or twice, about 40 minutes. Remove from oven; set aside to cool.

2. Over medium-high heat, heat a splash of olive oil in a small skillet. Add ancho chili and sauté until it puffs slightly and gets a shade darker, about 1 minute. Transfer to a bowl and cover with boiling water. Let stand until chili is softened, 15–30 minutes.

3. When vegetables are cool enough to handle, peel and seed tomatoes and red peppers, and roughly chop the onion. Seed the ancho chili. Place everything in a blender.

4. Over medium-high heat, heat another splash of olive oil in the skillet and add almonds. Cook until lightly toasted, about 1–2 minutes. Add almonds to blender.

5. To the blender, add ¼ cup olive oil, garlic, vinegar, bread, smoked paprika, and cayenne. Purée until it is smooth, but still rough textured.

6. Transfer Romesco Sauce to a bowl and season to taste with salt and pepper.

Jerk Sauce

Jerk is a fiery sauce that originates in Jamaica. It's supposed to be very spicy, so don't be shy about using those peppers.

Yields 1 cup

1. Heat the oil in a small skillet. Add the garlic and chili peppers and sauté until garlic begins to brown. Add allspice, cinnamon, and brown sugar. Cook, stirring constantly, until the sugar melts and mixture beings to clump. Remove from heat and let cool.

2. Put mixture into a blender. Add remaining ingredients and blend until it forms a smooth paste.

3. Refrigerate in an airtight container where it will keep for 2 weeks.

2 tablespoons olive oil
6 garlic cloves, peeled and finely minced
2 Scotch bonnet or habanero peppers, seeded and finely chopped
1 tablespoon ground allspice
1 teaspoon ground cinnamon
2 tablespoons brown sugar
1 teaspoon white pepper
1 tablespoon dried thyme
1 teaspoon salt
1 teaspoon ground ginger
4 scallions, roughly chopped
⅔ cup fresh lime juice
¼ cup red wine vinegar

🔥 VINEGARS

The word vinegar comes from the French vin aigre, *which means "sour wine." Throughout history, it has been one of the most important elements in food preservation. Vinegars come in all sorts of flavors—red wine, champagne, raspberry, balsamic—and can add both acidity and complexity to dishes.*

Ajvar

Ajvar (pronounced "AYE-var") is a roasted vegetable spread that's a staple of Serbian cuisine. You can serve Ajvar as a dip for chips, crackers, or flatbread. It also makes a nice addition to sandwiches. Try using smoked paprika for an extra flavor boost.

Yields about 2 cups

1 medium eggplant, cut into thick slices
2 red bell peppers, whole
5 cloves of garlic, whole and unpeeled
½ cup olive oil
½ teaspoon salt
1½ teaspoons hot paprika
½ teaspoon red pepper flakes
¼ teaspoon ground cayenne pepper
Black pepper, to taste
1–2 teaspoons fresh lemon juice, or to taste

1. Preheat the oven to 350°F. Place the eggplant, red bell peppers, and garlic on a baking sheet. Roast the vegetables for 1–2 hours until they are brown and soft (the eggplant should be collapsed), turning every 20 minutes.

2. Remove the vegetables from the oven and let cool. When the vegetables are cool, peel them. Discard the skins as well as the pepper seeds and core.

3. Roughly chop the vegetables and add to a blender or food processor.

4. Add the remaining ingredients and process until it forms a thick, smooth paste.

5. Store in an airtight container in the refrigerator for up to 2 weeks.

Red Garlic Mayonnaise

This spicy mayonnaise adds a kick to any sandwich!

Whisk together garlic, mayonnaise or soy mayo, and roasted pepper purée. Season with a pinch of salt, a squeeze of lemon, and cayenne.

Yields 1½ cups

2 cloves garlic, chopped very
   fine
1 cup mayonnaise or soy mayo
1 small red pepper, roasted,
   peeled, and puréed
Salt, to taste
½ lemon
Pinch of cayenne

Chipotle Mayo

This spicy mayo makes a great addition to sandwiches and burgers. You can easily double or triple this recipe, and feel free to use low-fat mayo or sour cream.

Yields 1 cup

½ cup mayonnaise
½ cup sour cream
2 cans chipotle chilies, finely chopped
Pinch of dried oregano leaves

1. In a medium bowl, combine the mayonnaise and sour cream.

2. Add the chopped chilies, along with a bit of the sauce from the can, and the oregano.

3. Stir all the ingredients until well blended.

4. Cover and refrigerate. Let it chill for at least an hour before use so the flavors can come together.

Chili-Orange Butter for Grilled Bread

The chili powder in this recipe gives this butter a kick that's absolutely delicious on grilled bread!

1. Pulse butter in a food processor until smooth. With machine running, add orange juice concentrate, honey, chili powder, and salt.

2. Spread or spoon onto grilled country bread.

Yields 8 (1 tablespoon) servings

8 ounces butter, room temperature

1 teaspoon orange juice concentrate

2 teaspoons dark honey

2 teaspoons New Mexico chili powder, or other chili powder

Pinch of salt

🌶 ADDED CHAR

Chefs have been melting flavored butters, called compound butters, over grilled items like portobello mushrooms for years, adding flavor and richness, while taking advantage of the savory natural juices cooked foods produce. They know that as the butter melts, it mixes with the intense char on the food's surface, making a sauce that capitalizes on the food's own unique character.

Fresh Tomato Chutney

For a change of pace, you can spread this pressure cooker Fresh Tomato Chutney over Indian chapati bread, flatbread, or pizza crust, then top with goat cheese or vegan mozzarella and bake.

Yields 4 cups

4 pounds ripe tomatoes, peeled
1" piece fresh ginger
3 cloves garlic, peeled and finely minced
1¾ cups white sugar
1 cup red wine vinegar
2 onions, diced
¼ cup golden raisins
¾ teaspoon ground cinnamon
½ teaspoon ground coriander
¼ teaspoon ground cloves
¼ teaspoon ground nutmeg
¼ teaspoon ground ginger
1 teaspoon chili powder
1 pinch paprika
1 tablespoon curry paste

1. Purée the peeled tomatoes and fresh ginger in a blender or food processor.

2. Pour the puréed tomato mixture into the pressure cooker. Stir in the remaining ingredients. Stir to mix, lock the lid into place, and cook at low pressure for 10 minutes. Remove from heat and allow pressure to release naturally. Refrigerate in a covered container until ready to use. Serve chilled or at room temperature.

❀ PEELING FRESH, VINE-RIPENED TOMATOES

Add enough water to a saucepan to cover the tomatoes; bring to a boil over medium-high heat. Use a slotted spoon to submerge the tomatoes in the boiling water for 1 minute, or until their skins begin to crack and peel. Use the slotted spoon to remove the tomatoes from the water and plunge them into ice water. The peelings will slip right off.

Green Tomato Chutney

If you want to take this spicy pressure cooker chutney down a notch, you can substitute two red bell peppers for the Anaheim and jalapeño peppers in this dish.

1. Put all ingredients in the pressure cooker; stir to mix. Lock on the lid and bring to low pressure. Cook on low pressure for 10 minutes. Remove from heat and allow pressure to release naturally.

2. Cool and refrigerate overnight before serving. Can be stored in a covered container in the refrigerator for 2 months.

Yields 5 cups

2 pounds green tomatoes, diced, with stems removed
1 white onion, quartered lengthwise, and thinly sliced
1 Anaheim pepper, diced
4 jalapeño peppers, diced
¼ cup dried currants
2 tablespoons fresh ginger, grated
¾ cup dark brown sugar, firmly packed
¾ cup white wine or white distilled vinegar
Pinch sea salt

Green Coriander Chutney

This bright green chutney gets an extra pop from the addition of grated coconut. It's very nice simply spread on toast.

Yields about 1 cup

1 bunch coriander (cilantro), stems included
3 or 4 sprigs of fresh mint
2 serrano chilies, seeded and roughly chopped
3 garlic cloves, peeled and roughly chopped
¼ cup unsweetened grated coconut
1 (1") piece of fresh ginger, peeled and chopped
Juice of 2 fresh lemons
½ teaspoon salt

1. Place all the ingredients in a blender or food processor and blend until smooth.

2. Pour chutney into a jar. It may seem a little thin, but will thicken into a paste.

3. Store in the refrigerator, where it will keep for up to 1 month.

🔥 CHUTNEY

Chutneys are condiments and spreads made from cooking down fruit that is flavored with spices. The word comes from the Sanskrit word catni *and originated as a South Asian food, though now it is used and made around the world. Chutneys can be made from almost any fruit or vegetable, but common ones found are mango, tomato, and tamarind.*

Mango Chutney

Sweet, sour, and spicy all at once, this chutney is great spread onto crackers.

1. Combine all the ingredients in a heavy-bottomed saucepan and let simmer over very low heat for 20–30 minutes, until it is very thick.

2. Remove chutney from heat and let cool.

3. When chutney is cooled, transfer to a glass jar and store, covered, in the refrigerator up to several weeks.

Yields about 2 cups

3 ripe yellow mangoes, peeled, pitted, and cut into ½" cubes
1 (2") piece fresh ginger, peeled and finely minced
2 garlic cloves, peeled and finely minced
½ teaspoon salt
½ teaspoon cayenne pepper
1 cup vinegar
¾ cup light brown sugar

Caribbean Relish

Think of this pressure cooker relish as hummus with a Caribbean flair.

Serves 12

1½ cups red or white kidney beans

7 cups water

2 teaspoons vegetable oil

Salt, to taste

2 tablespoons tahini paste

¾ cup crushed pineapple, drained

4 cloves garlic, minced

¼ teaspoon dried cumin

¼ teaspoon ground ginger

¼ teaspoon freshly ground white pepper

½ cup fresh cilantro, minced

1. Add the beans to the pressure cooker and pour 3 cups water over them, or enough to cover the beans completely. Cover and let soak overnight. Drain and return to the pressure cooker. Pour 4 cups water over the beans. Add the oil. Lock the lid into place. Bring to high pressure; maintain pressure for 10 minutes. Remove from heat and allow pressure to release naturally for 10 minutes.

2. Quick-release any remaining pressure. Remove the lid and, if the beans are cooked through, drain them. If additional cooking time is needed, lock the lid into place, return to high pressure, and cook for an additional 2–5 minutes.

3. Add the cooked beans, salt, tahini, pineapple, garlic, cumin, ginger, pepper, and cilantro to a blender or food processor. Pulse until mixed but still chunky. Transfer to a covered container and chill.

CHAPTER 3

Salads, Hors d'Oeuvres, and Snacks

SALADS

Southeast Asian Slaw

Madras Curry Dressing

Asian Cucumber Salad

Lentil Salad

Curried New Potato Salad

Chipotle Black Bean Salad

Tunisian Fried Pepper Salad

Spicy Rice Salad

Shiitake Mushroom Salad with Chilies

Black Bean Salad with Tapatío Vinaigrette

Cactus Salad

HORS D'OEUVRES AND SNACKS

Curry Dip

Baba Ghanoush

Jalapeño Cheese Dip

Chili-Cheese Dip

Frijole Dip

Texas Caviar

Guacamole

Hot and Spicy Hummus

Manchego-Potato Tacos with Pickled Jalapeños

Spicy Slow Cooker Buffalo Strips

Vegetable Gado-Gado

Spanish Sweet and Spicy Almonds

Potato Pakoras (Fritters)

Spicy White Bean–Citrus Dip

Black Bean Dip

Spiced Pecans

Cheese Soufflé

Marinated Feta Cheese

General Tso's Tofu

Spicy Tempeh Fajitas

Spicy Southwestern Corn Bread

Chiles Rellenos

Chalupas

Rajas Cooked in Beer

Southeast Asian Slaw

This crisp, lightly spiced salad is fine enough to roll in Asian-inspired wraps, and combines beautifully with jasmine rice cooked in coconut milk to make a unique taste.

Serves 4

¼ head (about ½ pound) Napa cabbage
½ carrot, grated
1 small red onion, julienne
1 small Thai (bird's eye) chili or jalapeño pepper, finely chopped
¼ cup chopped cilantro
Juice of 1 lime
1 tablespoon rice wine vinegar
1 teaspoon sugar
1 teaspoon vegetable oil
A few drops sesame oil
½ teaspoon salt

1. Shred the cabbage as fine as you possibly can, using a knife, mandoline, or slicing machine. Combine with carrot, onion, chili pepper, and cilantro.

2. Dress with lime, rice vinegar, sugar, vegetable oil, sesame oil, and salt; toss thoroughly.

3. Refrigerate for at least 30 minutes before serving.

Madras Curry Dressing

Perfect as a dip for crudités or a spread on sandwiches, this spicy dressing balances the sweetness of dried fruits with the complexity of Indian spices and light chili "heat."

1. In a small skillet, heat oil over medium heat for 1 minute. Add onion, bell pepper, and jalapeño. Cook until onion is translucent, about 2 minutes; add curry powder, coriander, turmeric, and cayenne. Cook 4 minutes more, stirring with a wooden spoon. Some of the spices may stick—this is not a problem. Remove from heat; allow to cool a few minutes. Drain the raisins.

2. In the bowl of a food processor, combine onion mixture and raisins. Pulse until smooth, scraping sides of bowl frequently. Add half of lime juice and the mayonnaise. Pulse to combine, then stir in cilantro. Adjust seasoning with salt, pepper, and remaining lime juice. Can be made up to 1 week in advance.

Yields about 1¼ cups

1 tablespoon oil
1 small red onion, finely chopped
2 tablespoons chopped red bell pepper
1 teaspoon finely chopped and seeded jalapeño pepper
2 tablespoons Madras curry powder
1 teaspoon ground coriander
1 teaspoon ground turmeric
¼ teaspoon cayenne pepper
1 tablespoon raisins, soaked in ½ cup warm water
Juice of 1 lime (about 2 tablespoons)
1 cup mayonnaise
2 tablespoons chopped cilantro
Salt and pepper, to taste

Asian Cucumber Salad

This refreshing, crisp dish is the perfect counterbalance with grilled tempeh, spicy corn fritters, and other hearty fare.

Serves 4

¼ cup rice wine vinegar
1 teaspoon sugar
1 teaspoon chopped jalapeño pepper
1 European-style long cucumber or 1 large regular cucumber
Sesame oil

1. Whisk together rice vinegar, sugar, and chopped jalapeño. If using a European cuke, it is not necessary to peel, but if using an American cuke, peel it. Halve the cucumber lengthwise; remove seeds. Slice seeded cucumber very thinly into half-moons. Combine with dressing, drizzle in a few drops of sesame oil, and toss to coat.

2. Marinate for at least 10 minutes before serving.

Lentil Salad

One of the oldest foods known to man, lentils have been found among the remains of prehistoric communities and are mentioned in the earliest books of the Bible. They cook more quickly than other beans, never require soaking, and taste great with the spicy flavors found in this Lentil Salad.

Wash lentils and pick through to take out any stones. Boil in 2 quarts of lightly salted water until tender but not broken up. Spread on a pan to cool. Combine with onions, scallions, and green pepper. Dress with remaining ingredients, and serve with a bed of dressed baby greens.

Serves 8

1 pound dried lentils
2 quarts lightly salted water
2 medium onions, finely chopped
3 scallions, chopped
1 green pepper, finely chopped
1 tablespoon toasted cumin powder
Pinch of cayenne pepper
Juice of 1 lemon (about ¼ cup)
2 tablespoons extra-virgin olive oil
Salt and freshly ground black pepper

Curried New Potato Salad

Simple to make, but with a complex, spicy taste, this Curried New Potato Salad is a great, attractive buffet item for a picnic lunch.

Serves 8

2 pounds red new potatoes, cut into bite-size chunks

Enough lightly salted water to cover potatoes

3 hard-boiled eggs, cut into bite-size chunks

1 recipe Madras Curry Dressing (see recipe in this chapter)

1 tablespoon chopped cilantro

Boil potatoes in lightly salted water until very tender, about 15 minutes; cool. Combine with eggs and curry dressing; toss to coat. Serve chilled, garnished with cilantro leaves.

Chipotle Black Bean Salad

There are actually five different varieties of black beans, but when you purchase black beans, they are often just labeled as black beans. No matter what type of black beans you buy, they'll still cook up great in the slow cooker for this spicy, fresh salad!

1. Add black beans, water, and salt to a 4-quart slow cooker. Cover and cook on high heat for about 5–6 hours. Check the beans at about 5 hours and continue cooking if necessary.

2. Once the beans are done, drain in a colander and allow to cool to room temperature.

3. Mix in the remaining ingredients and serve.

Serves 8

1 (16-ounce) bag dried black beans
Enough water to cover beans by 1"
2 teaspoons salt
1 tablespoon chipotle powder
2 teaspoons thyme
2 fresh tomatoes, diced
1 red onion, diced
¼ cup chopped cilantro

♦ PREPPING DRIED BEANS

Before cooking with dried beans, you must first rinse the beans, soak them overnight in a pot full of water, and then boil them for 10 minutes. They are then ready for Step 1 of the recipe.

Tunisian Fried Pepper Salad

This salad, which is also known as marmouma or chakchouka, makes an unexpected but delightful side dish or appetizer. Feel free to turn up the heat with more hot paprika. Serve it with crusty bread and, if you like, goat cheese.

Serves 6

4 tablespoons olive oil
4 red bell peppers, stemmed and seeded, cut into ½" pieces
5 garlic cloves, finely chopped
1½ pounds tomatoes, roughly chopped
1 teaspoon hot paprika
Salt and pepper, to taste
½ teaspoon red wine vinegar (optional)

1. Heat the olive oil in a frying pan. Add the pepper slices and fry over low heat, turning them every so often until they are soft.

2. Add the garlic and cook until the garlic is softened and the peppers are lightly browned.

3. Add the tomatoes, paprika, salt, and pepper. Give the whole mixture a gentle stir and then simmer, uncovered, until the tomatoes are reduced to a very thick consistency, about 20–25 minutes.

4. Taste the mixture. If it tastes too sweet, add the red wine vinegar.

5. Serve on top or alongside slices of crusty bread.

Spicy Rice Salad

This spicy salad is simple, but absolutely delicious!

1. Make the dressing by whisking together rice vinegar, vegetarian "fish" sauce, sesame oil, chili oil, and lime juice. Set aside.

2. Cook the rice. Fluff the rice with a fork, then transfer it to a large mixing bowl. Allow the rice to cool slightly.

3. Pour approximately ⅓ of the dressing over the rice and fluff to coat. Continue to fluff the rice every so often until it is completely cooled.

4. Add the green onions, carrots, red pepper, serrano chili pepper, mint, and cilantro to the rice. Toss with the remaining dressing.

5. To serve, place on individual plates and garnish with peanuts.

Yields 8 cups

½ cup rice vinegar
½ cup vegetarian "fish" sauce
¼ cup sesame oil
¼ cup chili oil
¼ cup lime juice
2 cups long-grain rice (preferably jasmine)
4–6 green onions, trimmed and thinly sliced
2 carrots, peeled and diced
1 sweet red pepper, seeded and diced
1 serrano chili pepper, seeded and minced
¼–½ cup chopped mint
¼–½ cup chopped cilantro
⅓ cup chopped unsalted peanuts

Shiitake Mushroom Salad with Chilies

This is a simple, spicy salad with plenty of heat and earthy mushroom flavor.

Serves 4

12 dried chiles de árbol, stemmed
2 tablespoons scallions, both green and white parts, thinly sliced
2 tablespoons sesame oil
2 tablespoons rice vinegar
2 tablespoons soy sauce
12 large shiitake mushrooms, stemmed and thinly sliced

1. Grind chilies in a spice grinder or food processor until they make a fine powder. Transfer to bowl and add scallions, oil, vinegar, and soy sauce. Set dressing aside.

2. Bring a pot of salted water to boil over high heat. Add mushrooms and cook until lightly chewy, about 4–5 minutes.

3. Drain mushrooms well. Transfer them to a kitchen towel or paper towels and squeeze out as much liquid as possible.

4. Put mushrooms in a bowl and pour dressing over top. Toss and let stand for 10 minutes before serving.

🌶 SHIITAKE MUSHROOMS

Of the many varieties of mushrooms around the world, shiitakes are most strongly associated with Asian cuisine. They're used throughout Japanese, Chinese, and Korean cooking. Pronounced "she-TAH-kay," the name is derived from the Japanese word for tree. They have a very strong, earthy flavor. You can find them fresh at most grocery stores, and also dried at many Asian markets.

Black Bean Salad with Tapatío Vinaigrette

Tapatío, cilantro, black beans, and cumin give this salad a fresh but decidedly south-of-the-border flavor.

1. Make the vinaigrette. Combine lime juice, salt, Tapatío, garlic, cumin, and olive oil in small bowl or jar. Stir or shake to combine. Taste and adjust seasonings to your liking.

2. Cook the quinoa. Wash it very thoroughly (if you do not wash quinoa before cooking it will have an unpleasant, bitter flavor), then put it in a saucepan with 1½ cups water. Bring it to a boil, then turn heat to low and let simmer for 12–15 minutes. Remove from heat and set aside to cool.

3. Combine quinoa, black beans, onion, tomatoes, carrot, and cilantro. Stir to combine.

4. Toss salad with ¼ cup of the Tapatío vinaigrette. Taste and adjust seasoning to your liking, adding more dressing, cumin, salt, or pepper as needed.

Serves 6

- ¼ cup fresh lime juice
- ¼ teaspoon kosher salt
- ½–1 teaspoon Tapatío hot sauce, depending on your taste
- 1 clove garlic, peeled and finely minced
- ¼ teaspoon ground cumin
- ¾ cup olive oil
- 1 cup quinoa, cooked
- 1½ cups water
- 1 (15-ounce) can of black beans, drained
- ½ red onion, finely chopped
- 2 cups cherry tomatoes, cut into quarters
- 1 large carrot, peeled and finely chopped
- ⅓ cup fresh cilantro leaves, finely chopped

🔥 QUINOA

Quinoa (pronounced "KEEN-wah") is a plant that has been cultivated in the Andes Mountains of South America since 3000 B.C. Ancient Incas called quinoa "the mother grain." It has a nutty flavor and varieties come in colors ranging from tan to red to black. Quinoa is growing in popularity, likely because it is highly nutritious. It can be used as a substitute for grains like rice, but contains high amounts of fiber.

Cactus Salad

Cactus leaves, called *nopales*, are a common salad ingredient in Mexico. They have a distinct crunch and texture similar to okra. If you're not sure about handling fresh *nopales*, you can also buy them jarred at most Mexican groceries.

Serves 2

2 large *nopal* (cactus) pads, available at Mexican or specialty grocery stores
½ large white onion, diced
2 medium tomatoes, cubed
4 sprigs fresh cilantro leaves, finely chopped
2 jalapeño peppers, seeded, and finely chopped
1 avocado, peeled, pitted, and cubed (optional)
Juice of 1 lime
Salt and pepper, to taste

1. Clean the *nopales* with a vegetable peeler or small paring knife. Using caution, remove all the thorns and bumps, paying special attention to the edges of the pads.

2. Cut the *nopales* into bite-size pieces and boil in water with a bit of salt for 25 minutes or until tender. Drain well.

3. Put *nopales* in a large bowl. Add all remaining ingredients, then stir gently until thoroughly mixed.

4. Put in the refrigerator until salad is cooled.

Curry Dip

Serve this spicy dip with toasted bread or your favorite cracker!

1. Put the oil in a small skillet over medium heat. Add onion, jalapeño, and red pepper; cook, stirring occasionally, until onion is translucent, about 5 minutes. Add curry powder, cumin, coriander, turmeric, cayenne, and salt. Cook a minute more, until spices are very fragrant. Add raisins and about 1 tablespoon of water. Remove from heat.

2. Transfer to a food processor. Chop on high speed for 30 seconds; scrape down sides of bowl with a rubber spatula. Add soy mayo and cilantro; process 30 seconds more, until smooth and even. Adjust seasonings with lemon, salt, and pepper, to taste.

Yields 2½ cups

1 teaspoon olive oil
½ cup finely chopped onion
½ medium jalapeño pepper, finely chopped (about 1 teaspoon)
2 teaspoons finely chopped red bell pepper
1 teaspoon Madras curry powder
1 teaspoon ground cumin
½ teaspoon ground coriander
½ teaspoon ground turmeric
Pinch of cayenne pepper
¼ teaspoon salt
1 tablespoon very fresh, soft raisins (or any raisins, soaked overnight in ½ cup water, drained)
1½ cups soy mayo
1 tablespoon chopped fresh cilantro
A few drops fresh lemon juice
Salt and pepper, to taste

Baba Ghanoush

Serve this hot and spicy Baba Ghanoush with wedges of warm pita bread.

Serves 4

2 cloves garlic, peeled
1 whole eggplant, roasted
   1 hour in a 400°F oven,
   cooled, pulp scooped out
1 tablespoon tahini
1½ teaspoons kosher salt
2–3 teaspoons toasted cumin
   powder
Juice of 2 lemons
¼ cup extra-virgin olive oil, plus
   a little extra for garnish
Freshly ground black pepper
Paprika and chopped parsley
   for garnish
Pita bread for dipping

1. In a food processor, chop the garlic until it sticks to the walls of the processor bowl. Add eggplant pulp, tahini, salt, cumin, and half of the lemon juice. Process until smooth, gradually drizzling in the olive oil. Season to taste with black pepper, additional salt, and lemon if necessary.

2. Spread onto plates, and garnish with a drizzle of extra-virgin olive oil, a few drops of lemon, a dusting of paprika, and some chopped parsley. Serve with wedges of warm pita bread.

Jalapeño Cheese Dip

To pump up the spice in this pressure cooker recipe, just add extra pickled jalapeños!

1. In the pressure cooker, soften butter or margarine over low heat and gradually add flour until you have a paste. Add milk or soymilk and stir until it has thickened and there are no lumps. Bring the mixture to a boil.

2. Add the cheeses and stir until smooth. Add the tomatoes and jalapeños and secure the lid on the pressure cooker. Cook on high until the pressure indicator rises. Lower heat and cook for 3 minutes. Allow the pressure to release and remove the lid. Add the lemon juice, salt, and pepper.

Serves 12

2 tablespoons butter or vegan margarine
2 tablespoons flour
1 cup milk or vegan soymilk
8 ounces shredded Cheddar cheese or vegan Cheddar such as Daiya Cheddar Style Shreds
8 ounces shredded Colby cheese or more vegan Cheddar
½ cup canned tomatoes
½ cup pickled jalapeños
2 tablespoons lemon juice
Salt and pepper, to taste

Chili-Cheese Dip

The perfect accompaniment for this spicy slow cooker dip is salty corn tortilla chips.

Serves 12

1 (15-ounce) can vegetarian chili
¼ cup diced onions
½ cup diced tomatoes
1 (8-ounce) package cream cheese or vegan cream cheese
1 cup shredded Cheddar cheese or vegan Cheddar
1 teaspoon garlic powder

1. In a 4-quart slow cooker, place all ingredients.

2. Stir gently; cover and heat on low for 1 hour.

🌶 VEGETARIAN CHILI

Most major grocery stores sell canned vegetarian chili. One of the easiest to find is Hormel Vegetarian Chili with Beans, which contains textured vegetable protein instead of meat.

Frijole Dip

For best results, serve this spicy slow cooker dip immediately after cooking or reheat if it cools. Keep in mind that if you make it the night before serving, you allow the spices time to mingle, which results in a spicier dish!

1. In a 4-quart slow cooker, add the beans, water, olive oil, onion, and garlic. Cover and cook over low heat for 1 hour.

2. Mash the beans until about ½ are smooth and ½ are still chunky.

3. Add all remaining ingredients; stir well, and cook for an additional 30 minutes.

Serves 12

2 (15-ounce) cans pinto beans, drained
1½ cups water
1 tablespoon olive oil
1 small onion, peeled and diced
3 cloves garlic, peeled and minced
1 cup diced tomatoes
1 teaspoon chipotle powder
½ teaspoon cumin
¼ cup fresh cilantro, finely chopped
Salt, to taste
1 cup Monterey jack cheese, grated, or vegan Monterey jack cheese

Texas Caviar

Prepare this pressure cooker dip up to two days in advance and store in a covered container in the refrigerator.

Yields 5 cups

1 cup dried black-eyed peas
8 cups water
1 pound cooked corn kernels
½ onion, diced
½ bell pepper, diced
1 pickled jalapeño, finely
  chopped
1 medium tomato, diced
2 tablespoons fresh chopped
  cilantro
¼ cup red wine vinegar
2 tablespoons olive oil
1 teaspoon salt
½ teaspoon ground black
  pepper
½ teaspoon ground cumin

1. Rinse and soak the black-eyed peas in 4 cups of water for 1 hour. Drain and rinse.

2. Add the black-eyed peas and remaining 4 cups of water to the pressure cooker. Lock the lid into place; bring to high pressure and maintain for 11 minutes. Remove from heat and allow pressure to release naturally.

3. Pour the drained black-eyed peas into a large mixing bowl; add all remaining ingredients and stir until combined. Refrigerate 1–2 hours before serving.

Guacamole

Serve this flavorful dip with tortilla chips, or as an accompaniment to spicy food.

With a mortar and pestle, or in a mixing bowl with a fork, mash together the garlic, onion, and jalapeño. Add the avocado and mash until it forms a chunky paste. Add lime juice, salt, pepper, and cilantro, and stir to combine. Garnish with chopped tomato if desired.

Serves 8

2 cloves garlic, chopped
¼ cup chopped red onion
1 small jalapeño pepper, finely chopped
4 ripe Hass avocados, halved, pitted, and scooped from the skin
2 tablespoons lime juice
½ teaspoon salt
Freshly ground black pepper, to taste
¼ cup chopped cilantro
1 plum tomato, seeded and chopped (optional)

Hot and Spicy Hummus

Hummus is delicious when served with wedges of warm pita bread!

Yields 2 cups

1 cup dried garbanzos (chickpeas), soaked overnight if desired, or 1 (16-ounce) can
2 cloves garlic, peeled
3 tablespoons tahini
½ teaspoon kosher salt
2–3 teaspoons toasted cumin powder
Juice of 1 lemon, divided in half
¼ cup extra-virgin olive oil, plus a little extra for garnish
Freshly ground black pepper
Paprika and chopped parsley for garnish
Pita bread for dipping

1. If using dried chickpeas, cook them in lightly salted water until very, very tender. If using canned chickpeas, drain and rinse them. In a food processor, chop the garlic until it sticks to the sides of the bowl. Add chickpeas, tahini, salt, cumin, and half of the lemon juice. Process until smooth, gradually drizzling in the olive oil. Add up to ¼ cup cold water to achieve a softer hummus if desired. Season to taste with black pepper, and additional salt and lemon, to taste.

2. Spread onto plates and garnish with extra-virgin olive oil, lemon juice, paprika, and chopped parsley. Serve with wedges of warm pita bread.

🔥 KOSHER SALT: THE CHEFS' SEASONING

Chefs know that judicious use of salt is essential to bring certain flavors to life. Almost all professional chefs, except those creating dishes for people with specific medical conditions, use some amount of salt in their cooking. In finer restaurants, the salt of choice in the kitchen is seldom the fine-powdered table salt most home cooks are familiar with. Instead, they use either complex-tasting crystal sea salt or coarse, flaky white salt known as "kosher" salt. It is so named because it is the type used for certain processes involved in the Jewish dietary laws, or "kashruth." It is available at most supermarkets.

Manchego-Potato Tacos with Pickled Jalapeños

Serve these tacos with salsa to boost up the spicy taste!

1. Spoon 1 tablespoon of mashed potato into the center of each tortilla. Flatten out the potatoes, leaving a 1" border. Lay 2 pieces of Manchego and 2 pieces pickled jalapeño onto each tortilla, and fold closed into a half-moon shape.

2. In a skillet over medium heat, melt half of the butter. Gently lay 4 of the tacos into the pan, and cook until nicely browned, about 3–4 minutes on each side. Drain on paper towels. Repeat with remaining tacos. Snip tacos in half before serving with salsa.

Serves 8

1 cup leftover mashed potatoes, or instant mashed potatoes, made firm

8 soft corn tortillas

¼ pound Spanish Manchego cheese or sharp Cheddar, cut into 16 small sticks

16 slices pickled jalapeño pepper (available in Mexican sections and ethnic specialty stores)

4 tablespoons unsalted butter

Spicy Slow Cooker Buffalo Strips

Most bottled buffalo wing sauces contain butter, so if you're vegan, check the label.

Serves 6

⅓ cup butter or vegan margarine

⅓ cup hot sauce

1 tablespoon vinegar

1 teaspoon garlic powder

2 (7-ounce) packages Gardein Chick'n Strips

1. Place the butter or margarine in a small bowl and microwave for 30 seconds, or until melted.

2. Add the hot sauce, vinegar, and garlic powder and stir well.

3. In a 4-quart slow cooker, add the prepared hot sauce and Chick'n Strips and cook over low heat for 1 hour.

🔥 SERVING STRIPS

Faux buffalo chicken strips can be added to sandwiches or salads, but if you'd like to serve them as an appetizer or snack, place in a small basket lined with parchment paper and add sides of celery sticks, carrot sticks, and vegan ranch dressing.

Vegetable Gado-Gado

This appetizer of vegetables with a spicy peanut sauce is Indonesian in origin.

1. Blanch all the vegetables quickly in lightly salted boiling water; plunge immediately into ice-cold water to stop the cooking process. Drain and arrange in an attractive pattern on a serving platter.

2. Combine peanut butter, honey, salt, cayenne, and lime juice in a food processor or mixing bowl; pulse or whisk together until smooth. Gradually work in coconut milk until a saucy consistency is reached. Adjust consistency further, if desired, with hot water. Serve as a dipping sauce with blanched vegetables.

Serves 8

16 each: 2-bite carrot sticks, broccoli florets, trimmed green beans, batons of yellow bell pepper and/or yellow summer squash, and assorted other vegetables

½ cup smooth peanut butter

¼ cup honey

¼ teaspoon salt

⅛ teaspoon cayenne pepper

1 tablespoon lime juice

¾ cup (6 ounces) coconut milk

Spanish Sweet and Spicy Almonds

Almonds grow everywhere in Spain, so these are a tapas menu staple.

Serves 4

2 tablespoons extra-virgin olive oil
1 teaspoon salt
1 teaspoon pimenton (Spanish paprika) or hot paprika
¼ teaspoon cayenne pepper
¼ cup honey
1 cup whole almonds, skin on

1. Preheat oven to 350°F.

2. Combine the olive oil, salt, paprika, cayenne pepper, and honey in a bowl with a fork. Add the almonds and stir to coat.

3. Pour the coated almonds onto a baking sheet lined with nonstick foil and separate them into individual nuts with a fork.

4. Bake for 10 minutes, stir the nuts around, and bake another 5 minutes. Let cool on the foil and then break them into individual nuts and store them in a tin with a tight-fitting lid.

🔥 EXTRA ALMOND SPICE

While the almonds are still warm, sprinkle them with a mixture of equal parts sugar and salt and a big pinch of cayenne pepper and ground cinnamon. Then let them cool. They will have a frosty coating of spicy crystals when they harden.

Potato Pakoras (Fritters)

Serve these feisty fritters immediately with chutney for dipping.

1. In a food processor or blender, pulse flour, oil, cumin, cayenne or paprika, turmeric, and salt 3 or 4 times until fluffy. With blade spinning, gradually add water, processing for 2–3 minutes until smooth. Adjust consistency by adding water until the mixture is slightly thicker than the consistency of heavy cream. Cover and set aside for 10 minutes.

2. Heat fry oil to 350°F. Dip potato slices into batter one by one, and slip them into the fry oil in batches of 6 or 7. Fry 4–5 minutes each side, until golden brown and cooked through.

Serves 8

1¼ cups sifted chickpea flour
2 teaspoons vegetable oil
1½ teaspoons ground cumin
½ teaspoon cayenne or paprika
¼ teaspoon turmeric
2½ teaspoons salt
Approximately ½ cup cold water
1 large or 2 medium baking
   potatoes (about 8 ounces),
   peeled, then sliced into ⅛"
   pieces
Oil for frying

Spicy White Bean–Citrus Dip

Tangy, spicy, unique, and easy to throw together, this stupendous dip is perfect for tortilla chips, fried plantains, raw vegetables, or as a spread in a burrito.

Serves 12

2 (15-ounce) cans white navy beans, drained and rinsed
¼ cup sour cream
1 tablespoon orange juice concentrate
1 teaspoon chipotle purée or hot pepper sauce
1 teaspoon lime juice
Zest of 1 orange, grated
½ teaspoon salt
½ cup diced white onions
1 tablespoon chopped cilantro

Purée the beans, sour cream, orange juice concentrate, chipotle or hot pepper sauce, lime juice, orange zest, and salt in a food processor until smooth. Add onions and cilantro; mix with a rubber spatula until combined.

Black Bean Dip

To give this pressure cooker dip an extra kick, you can substitute canned jalapeño peppers for the mild green chilies or add 2 teaspoons of chipotle powder.

1. Add the beans and water to a container; cover and let the beans soak 8 hours at room temperature.

2. Add the oil and the onion to the pressure cooker; sauté for 3 minutes or until the onion is soft. Add the garlic and sauté for 30 seconds.

3. Drain the beans and add them to the pressure cooker along with the tomatoes, chilies, chili powder, and oregano. Stir well. Lock the lid into place. Bring to high pressure; maintain pressure for 12 minutes. Remove from heat and allow pressure to release naturally for 10 minutes.

4. Quick-release any remaining pressure. Remove the lid. Transfer the cooked beans mixture to a food processor or blender. Add the cilantro and process until smooth. Taste for seasoning; add salt if desired.

5. Transfer the dip to a bowl. Stir in the cheese. Serve warm.

Serves 12

1 cup dried black beans
2 cups water
1 tablespoon olive oil
1 small onion, peeled and diced
3 cloves garlic, peeled and minced
1 (14½-ounce) can diced tomatoes
2 (4-ounce) cans mild green chilies, finely chopped
1 teaspoon chili powder
½ teaspoon dried oregano
¼ cup fresh cilantro, finely chopped
Salt, to taste
1 cup Monterey jack cheese, grated, or vegan Monterey jack cheese, such as Follow Your Heart Vegan Gourmet Monterey Jack Cheese Alternative

---

🔥 OTHER BEAN OPTIONS

Bean dips are delicious when made with a variety of dried beans. To complement the flavors in this recipe, use black beans, pinto beans, or white beans. If you're pressed for time, use canned beans instead of dried beans, but be sure to drain the liquid first.

Spiced Pecans

These pecans are great if you like a little spice in your life.

Yields 3 cups

1 ounce (2 tablespoons)
  unsalted butter
1 pound whole, shelled pecans
2 tablespoons light soy sauce
1 tablespoon hoisin sauce
A few drops of hot pepper sauce

1. Heat oven to 325°F. Melt butter in a large skillet. Add nuts; cook, tossing occasionally, until nuts are well coated. Add soy sauce, hoisin sauce, and hot pepper sauce; cook 1 minute more. Stir to coat thoroughly.

2. Spread nuts into a single layer on a baking sheet. Bake until all liquid is absorbed and nuts begin to brown. Remove from oven. Cool before serving.

Cheese Soufflé

This spicy soufflé can be prepared in advance and kept in the refrigerator for up to an hour before baking, making it perfect for when guests come over.

1. Heat oven to 475°F. Butter a 10" soufflé dish and coat the inside with flour. Melt ½ cup butter in a double boiler or a steel bowl set over a pot of simmering water. Add the flour, salt, paprika, and cayenne or pepper sauce; mix well. Gradually stir in the milk with a stiff whisk or wooden spoon. Cook, stirring constantly, until the mixture has become very thick. Stir in the cheese, and continue stirring until all cheese is melted. Remove from heat.

2. Beat the yolks until they are lemon-colored, then gradually stir them into the cheese sauce. In a very clean bowl, whip the egg whites until they are stiff, but not dry. Gently fold them into the cheese sauce, and then pour this batter into the soufflé dish. At this point, the soufflé may be covered and refrigerated for up to 1 hour, or baked right away.

3. Bake at 475°F for 10 minutes. Reduce heat to 400°F, and bake for 25 minutes more. Serve immediately.

Serves 6

½ cup unsalted butter
½ cup flour
½ teaspoon table salt
½ teaspoon paprika
Dash of cayenne or pepper sauce
2 cups milk
½ pound sharp Cheddar cheese, diced
8 large eggs, separated

Marinated Feta Cheese

Serve this with crusty bread or crackers for a crowd-pleasing appetizer. It tastes best if you let it marinate overnight.

Serves 4 as an appetizer

8 ounces feta cheese

1 red serrano or jalapeño pepper (seeded if you like), finely chopped

2 garlic cloves, peeled and minced

4 scallions, both green and white parts, thinly sliced

½ bunch fresh parsley leaves, finely chopped

6 tablespoons olive oil

1. Chop feta cheese into small cubes. Place in a bowl.

2. Combine chili, garlic, scallions, parsley, and olive oil in a bowl.

3. Pour marinade over feta cheese, cover, and put in the refrigerator. Let it marinate for at least 4 hours, overnight if possible.

4. Pull out of refrigerator and let cheese warm to room temperature before serving.

🔥 FETA CHEESE

Feta is a salty, crumbly cheese that is synonymous with Greek cuisine. It's used in every imaginable way in Greece: in salads, as a table cheese, in savory pastries, and even drizzled with honey. While many types of similar cheese purport to be feta, since 2002 it's been European law that feta is a "protected designation of origin" product. In order to truly be called feta, a cheese must be produced in Greece and made from only sheep's or goat's milk.

General Tso's Tofu

The combination of sweet and spicy is what makes this dish a hit at Chinese restaurants across the country.

Add all ingredients to a 4-quart slow cooker. Cover and cook on high heat for 4 hours.

Serves 2

1 (16-ounce) package of extra-firm tofu, pressed and cubed
1 cup water
2 tablespoons cornstarch
2 cloves garlic, minced
1 teaspoon ginger, minced
⅛ cup sugar
2 tablespoons soy sauce
⅛ cup white wine vinegar
⅛ cup sherry
2 teaspoons cayenne pepper
2 tablespoons vegetable oil
2 cups broccoli, chopped

Spicy Tempeh Fajitas

Add a dollop of sour cream and salsa to finish off each of these spicy fajitas.

Serves 4

1 (13-ounce) package tempeh, cut into bite-size pieces
2 cloves garlic, minced
1 teaspoon fresh ginger, minced
¼ cup soy sauce
1 cup water
1 tablespoon olive oil
½ teaspoon chili powder
¼ teaspoon chipotle powder
¼ teaspoon black pepper
½ onion, sliced
½ green bell pepper, sliced
1 jalapeño, minced
½ cup mushrooms, sliced
8–12 corn tortillas
1 tomato, diced
¼ cup cilantro, chopped
1 lime, cut into wedges

1. Add the tempeh, garlic, ginger, soy sauce, water, olive oil, chili powder, chipotle powder, black pepper, onion, green bell pepper, jalapeño, and mushrooms to a 4-quart slow cooker. Cover and cook on low heat for 6 hours.

2. Serve the fajitas on the tortillas and garnish with tomato, cilantro, and lime.

Spicy Southwestern Corn Bread

European settlers were introduced to corn by Native Americans, and soon began using cornmeal in bread recipes. This smoky corn bread puts their bread to shame!

1. Heat oven to 400°F. In a large mixing bowl, combine the cornmeal, sugar, flour, baking powder, baking soda, and salt. Mix thoroughly with a stiff wire whisk or spoon to combine well and break up any lumps. In a separate mixing bowl, mix the buttermilk, oil, melted butter, eggs, jalapeños, and chipotle; whisk well to combine. Fold the cornmeal mixture into the buttermilk mixture in 3 additions, mixing only as much as necessary to combine ingredients. Pour the batter into 2 (9" × 5") loaf pans or 1 (9" × 13") baking dish. It is not necessary to grease the pans.

2. Bake until the top springs back when pressed and a toothpick comes out clean when inserted into the center. Cool 10 minutes before turning onto a rack to cool completely.

Yields 2 loaves

4½ cups fine cornmeal
1 cup sugar
2 cups flour
4 tablespoons baking powder
1 tablespoon baking soda
4 teaspoons table salt
3½ cups buttermilk
1 cup oil
1 cup (2 sticks) melted butter
6 eggs
1½ tablespoons chopped jalapeño peppers
2 tablespoons puréed chipotle peppers in adobo

Chiles Rellenos

These battered and fried chiles stuffed with cheese are a guaranteed favorite. To prep the chiles, simply blister them under the broiler for a few minutes on each side, then remove stems, seeds, and skin.

Serves 4

12 Anaheim or poblano chiles, charred and peeled
1 pound mild, melting cheese like Cheddar or Monterey jack, cut into strips
1 cup milk
1 cup all-purpose flour
1 egg, beaten
1 teaspoon baking powder
1 teaspoon baking soda
1 teaspoon salt
2–3 cups canola oil
½ cup all-purpose flour for coating

1. Stuff each pepper with a strip of cheese. Set aside.

2. In a small bowl, combine milk, 1 cup of flour, egg, baking powder, baking soda, salt, and canola oil. Mix well to make a batter.

3. Fill a heavy frying pan with about 1" of oil and heat over medium-high heat.

4. Spread the ½ cup of flour on a plate. When oil is hot, dust each stuffed chili in the flour, then dip in the egg batter. Gently drop chiles in oil.

5. Fry chiles until lightly browned on both sides. Remove to a plate covered with a paper towel to absorb excess oil.

Chalupas

These make a great, quick snack and are an easy way to use up leftover salsa. Use your favorite homemade salsa or, if you prefer, salsa from a jar.

1. Heat oil in a skillet. Place tortillas in pan and fry until they begin to crisp. Flip the tortillas.

2. With the tortillas still in the pan, add a heaping tablespoon of salsa, and some chopped onion, as well as shredded cheese if desired.

3. Turn the heat to low, cover, and let chalupas cook until toppings are heated through and optional cheese is melted. Serve.

Serves 4

Vegetable oil, for frying
8 small corn tortillas
2 cups of your salsa of choice
1 onion, finely chopped
Shredded cheese such as
    Monterey jack or Cheddar,
    or crumbled queso fresco
    (optional)

🌶 CHALUPAS

Chalupas, or little boats, are another Mexican staple that has endless variations, depending on the region. Typically, though, they are small tortillas that are loaded with salsa and toppings like vegetables, and cheese, to make a light snack. Chalupa toppings are limited only by your imagination.

Rajas Cooked in Beer

Who wouldn't love chili peppers cooked in beer and smothered with cheese? This is a Holy Trinity for many and a guaranteed crowd pleaser.

Serves 4

3 tablespoons vegetable oil
1 cup white onions, thinly sliced
Salt and pepper, to taste
6 poblano or Anaheim chilies, roasted, peeled, seeded, and cut into thin strips (rajas)
1 cup strong beer (no Corona here; use a darker lager)
¾ cup medium Cheddar cheese, shredded

1. Heat the oil in a skillet. Add the onions, salt, and pepper, and cook over low-medium heat until the onions turn soft and translucent, about 3–4 minutes.

2. Add the rajas, stir, cover the pan, and continue to cook until the chilies are tender.

3. Add the beer and continue cooking, uncovered, until it has been absorbed by the rajas.

4. Turn the heat to low, spread the cheese on top, cover, and cook until cheese is heated through and melted, about 3 minutes. Serve immediately.

CHAPTER 4

Salsas and Spice Mixes

SALSAS

Simple Salsa

Rancheros Salsa

Pressure Cooker Tomatillo Salsa

Pico de Gallo

Roasted Tomatillo Salsa

Mango Habanero Salsa

Chile de Árbol Salsa

Pineapple Salsa

Raw Tomatillo Salsa

Smoky Chipotle Salsa

Peanut Salsa

Creamy Pumpkin Seed and Habanero
Salsa

Mixed Chili Salsa

Salsa Ranchera

Roasted Corn Salsa

Guajillo Salsa

Avocado Salsa

Super Spicy Salsa

Zesty Black Bean Salsa

Black Bean Salsa

SPICES

Homemade Chili Powder

Berbere

Creole Seasoning Blend

Adobo Seasoning

Curry Powder

Ras El Hanout

Baharat

Simple Salsa

This simple spicy condiment pairs magnificently with burritos, tacos, empanadas, tortilla chips, and all kinds of other Mexican savories.

Yields 1 cup

2 large tomatoes
1 small onion, finely diced
1 or 2 jalapeño peppers, finely chopped
½ teaspoon fresh-squeezed lime juice
Salt and freshly ground black pepper
½ teaspoon chipotle purée (optional)

Quarter the tomatoes. Cut out the inside viscera; reserve. Cut the remaining petals into a fine dice. Purée the insides in a food processor until smooth. Toss together with the tomato dice, the diced onion, jalapeños, lime juice, salt, pepper, and chipotle if using. Keeps in the refrigerator for 2 days, but is best used the day it's made.

Rancheros Salsa

This salsa, the best part of Huevos Rancheros (see Chapter 1), freezes exceptionally well. Consider making a double batch and storing half for later.

In a large, heavy-bottomed pot, heat the oil over medium-high heat until hot but not smoky. Add onion, peppers, and plum tomatoes; cook 5 minutes until onion is translucent. In a food processor, purée garlic, diced tomatoes, and tomatillos; add to onion mixture. Cook 5 minutes more. Add chilies, chipotle, jalapeño, and cilantro; stir in orange juice concentrate, cumin, oregano, cinnamon, salt, and pepper. Cook 5 minutes more.

Yields 4 cups

2 tablespoons olive oil
1 medium white onion, roughly chopped
1 red bell pepper, roughly chopped
1 green bell pepper, roughly chopped
4 plum tomatoes, seeded and roughly chopped
1 tablespoon chopped garlic (about 4 cloves)
1 (14-ounce) can diced tomatoes in tomato purée
1 (7-ounce) can tomatillos, drained
1 (7-ounce) can green chilies, rinsed, drained, and roughly chopped
1 teaspoon chipotle purée
1 jalapeño pepper, seeded, finely chopped
¼ cup chopped cilantro
1 tablespoon frozen orange juice concentrate
1 teaspoon ground cumin, toasted in a dry pan until fragrant
1 teaspoon dried oregano
¼ teaspoon ground cinnamon
Salt and pepper, to taste

Pressure Cooker Tomatillo Salsa

Serve this Pressure Cooker Tomatillo Salsa with corn tortilla chips or as an accompaniment to Black Bean Dip (see Chapter 3).

Serves 8

1 pound tomatillos, paper removed

Water, as needed

2 jalapeños, stemmed, seeded, and chopped

½ onion, chopped

½ cup cold water

½ cup chopped cilantro

2 teaspoons salt

1. Cut the tomatillos in half and then place in the pressure cooker. Add enough water to cover the tomatillos.

2. Lock the lid into place; bring to high pressure and maintain for 2 minutes. Remove from heat and allow pressure to release naturally.

3. Add the drained, cooked tomatillos, jalapeños, onion, and cold water to a food processor or blender. Blend until well combined. Add the cilantro and salt and pulse until combined. Chill the salsa before serving.

🌶 TOMATILLO

Tomatillo is the small yellowish or green fruit of a Mexican ground cherry. Surprisingly, it is not a variety of tomato.

Pico de Gallo

This is a classic, fresh salsa that's easy to throw together just minutes before eating. This salsa tastes best in summer, when tomatoes are at their juiciest and most flavorful. For more spice, don't seed the chili peppers.

1. Combine all the ingredients in a bowl and mix thoroughly.

2. If there is time, let it sit in the refrigerator for 20 minutes.

Yields 2½ cups

1 white onion, finely chopped

4 ripe tomatoes, seeded and finely chopped

3 jalapeño peppers, seeded and finely chopped

½ cup cilantro leaves, finely chopped

1 tablespoon fresh lime juice

Salt, to taste

🔥 PICO DE GALLO: WHAT'S IN A NAME?

Pico de Gallo translates literally to "the beak of the rooster." The exact reason why is unknown, though perhaps it's because the red of the tomatoes is reminiscent of the bird's beak. Pico de Gallo is also beloved because it contains the three colors of the Mexican flag: red, white, and green.

Roasted Tomatillo Salsa

This is a relatively simple salsa, but taking the time to roast the tomatillos, chilies, garlic, and scallions gives the salsa an extra smoky and charred flavor that is well worth the extra time.

Yields about 2½ cups

1 pound tomatillos
2 garlic cloves
3 scallions
3 dried chiles de árbol
1 handful cilantro
Dried oregano, to taste
Salt, to taste

1. Remove the papery husks from the tomatillos and wash thoroughly.

2. Peel the garlic, but leave the cloves whole. Trim the root ends off the scallions.

3. On a comal or nonstick skillet, roast the tomatillos, chilies, garlic, and scallions until the tomatillos are softened and blackened.

4. Put all the vegetables into a blender with the cilantro, oregano, and salt. Blend until smooth.

5. Store in an airtight container in the refrigerator where it will keep for up to 2 weeks.

🌶 WHAT IS A COMAL?

A comal is a smooth, flat griddle, usually cast iron, used throughout Mexico and Latin America to cook tortillas, toast spices, and roast chilies and vegetables. In many cultures, the comal is handed down from generation to generation, with the idea that the comal becomes better and more seasoned with age. If you don't have a comal, no worries—a cast-iron pan will do.

Mango Habanero Salsa

This is a great salsa to enjoy in the summer. The juicy sweet mango offers a nice contrast to the ultrahot habanero pepper.

1. Set oven to broil. Place a rack 6" from the heat source. Put the oil, garlic, tomatillos, tomatoes, bell peppers, chili, and onion in a large bowl and toss.

2. Transfer the ingredients to a foil-lined baking sheet. Broil them, turning a few times, until they are charred and blistered, about 10 minutes.

3. Transfer all but the peppers and chilies to a bowl; let cool. Continue broiling the peppers and chilies until soft, 3–5 minutes longer. Remove chilies from oven and let them steam in a covered bowl for a few minutes.

4. Peel the garlic. Stem, seed, and peel peppers and chilies. Transfer all the roasted vegetables to a blender or food processor. Process until finely chopped.

5. Transfer the salsa to a bowl and stir in cilantro, lime juice, and mango. Season with salt.

Yields about 4 cups

3 tablespoons canola oil
3 whole cloves garlic, unpeeled
3 tomatillos, husked and washed
3 tomatoes, cored
1 red bell pepper
1 yellow bell pepper
1 orange habanero chili
1 medium red onion, finely chopped
¼ cup chopped cilantro leaves
¼ cup fresh lime juice
1 large mango, peeled, pitted, and cut into ¼" cubes
Kosher salt, to taste

Chile de Árbol Salsa

Chiles de árbol are a staple in many salsas because of their strong heat and naturally subtle, smoky flavor. This salsa puts those flavors at the forefront.

Yields 2 cups

½ pound Roma tomatoes
½ pound tomatillos, husked and washed
1 cup (between 30–40) chiles de árbol
½ bunch cilantro, leaves only, roughly chopped
1 medium white onion, chopped
4 garlic cloves, peeled and lightly smashed
2 cups water
1 teaspoon salt

1. Set oven to broil. Place tomatoes and tomatillos on a baking sheet. Broil, turning occasionally, until they are charred, 10–12 minutes. Transfer to a saucepan.

2. Add the remaining ingredients into saucepan. Bring mixture to a boil and cook until the onion is soft, about 12 minutes.

3. Transfer the sauce to a blender or food processor. Purée until smooth.

4. Strain the salsa into a bowl.

5. Store leftover salsa in the refrigerator, where it will keep for about a week.

Pineapple Salsa

Another great tropical salsa that's especially nice in the summer. If you can, let it sit for thirty minutes before serving to give all the flavors time to mix.

1. Toss all the ingredients together in a large bowl and mix well.

2. Serve immediately or cover and chill until ready to use.

Yields 2 cups

2 cups diced fresh pineapple
½ cup chopped cilantro
¼ cup red onion, finely chopped
1 serrano pepper, seeded and
  finely chopped
Juice and zest of 1 lime
¼ teaspoon kosher salt

Raw Tomatillo Salsa

This simple salsa, called *cruda*, is probably the easiest way to make a salsa from tomatillos. This sauce may seem a bit thin at first, but it will thicken as it stands.

Yields 1½ cups

1 pound (around 20) tomatillos, husked and washed
4 serrano chilies, seeded and roughly chopped
1 cup cilantro leaves and stems, roughly chopped
1 large garlic clove, peeled and roughly chopped
Salt, to taste

1. Put the tomatillos in a small pan, just barely cover them with water, and bring to a simmer. Simmer for about 10 minutes or until they are softened. Drain, but reserve a bit of the cooking water.

2. Combine ½ cup of the cooking water, chilies, cilantro, and garlic in a blender. Blend until almost smooth.

3. Add the cooked tomatillos in small batches, blending briefly after each one. The sauce should be chunky and rough.

4. Transfer to a bowl and add salt, to taste.

🌶 TOMATILLOS

Tomatillos, called tomates verdes *("green tomatoes") in Spanish, are not the same thing as green, unripe tomatoes. While they are in the same family, they are a different genus. Tomatillos grow surrounded by an inedible, paper-like "husk" that must be discarded before cooking.*

Smoky Chipotle Salsa

Chipotles add a surprise smoky flavor to this salsa, which also has plenty of sweetness from roasted tomatoes. Serve this as a table salsa with chips for a nice change of pace.

1. Roast tomatoes, onion, chilies, and garlic on a comal or cast-iron skillet until they are nearly blackened.

2. Place the vegetables and chilies in a blender and add a little water. Blend until smooth. Season with salt, to taste.

Yields about 2 cups

8 medium red tomatoes
1 yellow onion, halved
4 dried chipotle chilies
2 cloves garlic, peeled
½–1 cup water
Salt, to taste

Peanut Salsa

This unusual salsa originates on the Gulf Coast of Mexico. Spread this hot sauce on top of warm tortillas or rice.

Yields 2 cups

1 cup roasted unsalted peanuts, shelled
2 cups water, separated
4 canned chipotle peppers in adobo, roughly chopped
2 garlic cloves, peeled and roughly chopped
2 black peppercorns
2 cloves
2 tablespoons vegetable oil
Salt, to taste

1. Grind the peanuts in a coffee grinder or food processor until they are a fine powder.

2. Put ½ cup of water into the blender, along with the chilies, garlic, and spices. Blend well.

3. Heat the vegetable oil in a skillet, then fry the blended ingredients in it for 4 minutes, stirring constantly so they do not stick to the bottom. Gradually stir in the ground peanuts and cook for another 2 minutes.

4. Add the rest of the water and salt and continue cooking, stirring and scraping the bottom of the pan, for another 5 minutes.

Creamy Pumpkin Seed and Habanero Salsa

This salsa, called *sikil pak*, is a traditional Mayan recipe from the Yucatan Peninsula. It's incredibly creamy, yet there is no trace of dairy. Be careful when handling the roasted habanero here—consider gloves!

1. Toast the *pepitas* in a dry, hot skillet or in the oven until golden brown.

2. Char the tomatoes, onion, and habanero on a comal or cast-iron skillet until they are softened and a little black, about 5 minutes. Carefully seed and roughly chop the habanero.

3. Put all the ingredients into a food processor or blender. Pulse until well blended. The salsa should be thick and creamy. Add a little water to thin if necessary.

Yields 1½ cups

1 cup pumpkin seeds (*pepitas*), toasted
3 tomatoes
½ large white onion, thickly sliced
1 habanero chili
½ cup cilantro leaves
Salt, to taste
Water as needed

Mixed Chili Salsa

This raw salsa is bright and colorful. If you are lucky enough to live near a market that sells a variety of chilies, be sure to make this. Feel free to vary it with whatever chilies are fresh and available.

Yields 1½ cups

1 poblano chili, seeded and finely chopped
1 red jalapeño, seeded and finely chopped
2 yellow chilies (such as a güero or Anaheim), seeded and finely chopped
2 serrano chilies, seeds intact, finely chopped
½ white onion, finely chopped
2 tomatoes, seeded and finely chopped
3 tablespoons fresh lime juice
½ teaspoon dried oregano
Salt, to taste

1. Mix all the ingredients together in a nonreactive bowl.

2. Set aside for 1 hour before serving.

🔥 GÜERO

Güero chilies are medium-hot peppers that are a yellow color. They are also sometimes called goldspike chilies. Güero translates from Spanish to "blonde," though it is also called out on the streets in Mexico as a generic nickname (not necessarily derogatively) for light-haired or light-skinned tourists.

Salsa Ranchera

Here's a salsa for cheese lovers. This warm, spicy salsa is great served as an appetizer with warm tortillas or chips.

1. Heat oil in a skillet. Add the garlic and sauté, then add the chilies and onion. Cook them at low-medium heat until the onion is just beginning to brown.

2. Add the Vegetable Stock and cook over medium heat until the onion and chilies are softened and thoroughly cooked. Add salt, to taste.

3. Place the cheese on top and cover the pan.

4. Serve as soon as the cheese is melted.

Yields 1½ cups

3 tablespoons vegetable oil
2 garlic cloves, finely chopped
2 cups jalapeños, seeded, and cut into very fine strips
2 cups white onion, finely sliced
1 cup Vegetable Stock (see Chapter 5) (you can also use water, though broth adds more flavor)
Salt, to taste
8 ounces queso fresco or mild Cheddar

🔥 QUESO FRESCO

Queso fresco translates to "fresh cheese." It has a crumbly texture and sharp flavor that is reminiscent of a mild feta. Be sure to get whole-milk queso fresco because it will melt better. Queso fresco is also great crumbled over tacos.

Roasted Corn Salsa

This is a great spicy salsa to make in summer, when corn on the cob is bursting with sweetness. You can serve with chips or put it on tacos, but it's also hearty enough to be a side dish.

Yields 3½ cups

3 ears of fresh corn
4 scallions, white and green parts separated and thinly sliced
2 tablespoons unsalted butter
2 cloves garlic, peeled and minced
1½ teaspoons kosher salt, separated
1½ teaspoons ground cumin, separated
1 teaspoon chili powder, separated
Black pepper, to taste
2 plum tomatoes, seeded and finely diced
2 fresh jalapeños, with seeds, finely diced

1. Shuck the corn cobs and shave the corn kernels from the cob. Heat a dry, large cast-iron skillet over medium-high heat and pan-roast corn, stirring occasionally, until golden brown, about 8–9 minutes. Transfer to a bowl.

2. Cook the white parts of scallions in butter with garlic, 1 teaspoon of salt, ½ teaspoon each of cumin and chili powder, and a few pinches of black pepper. Cook until scallions are tender, about 3 minutes.

3. Remove pan from heat and stir in corn, tomatoes, jalapeños, green parts of scallions, and remaining amounts of spices.

4. Transfer to bowl. Serve warm or chill in the refrigerator before serving.

Guajillo Salsa

This is a salsa of medium heat, with plenty of nice chili flavor from the guajillos. You can serve it as a table salsa or heat it with two tablespoons of chili oil to make a hot sauce.

1. Remove the stems from the guajillos and lightly toast them on a comal or cast-iron skillet. Transfer them to a bowl and cover with hot water. Let them sit for at least 15 minutes.

2. When the chilies are softened, remove them from the water and chop roughly. Save a bit of the chili soaking water.

3. Purée the chilies with the remaining ingredients until the mixture forms a paste. Add a little chili water to thin if necessary.

Yields 3 cups

½ pound dried guajillo chilies
3 cups water
5 large cloves of garlic, roasted
1 teaspoon ground cumin
1 teaspoon kosher salt
½ pound Roma tomatoes
2 teaspoons toasted pumpkin seeds
⅓ cup apple cider vinegar
1 teaspoon dried oregano

❋ PUMPKIN SEEDS

Called pepitas *in Spanish, pumpkin seeds are commonly used in Mexican cuisine as a thickener for sauces. Along with adding body to salsas and moles, pumpkin seeds add a warm, nutty flavor to dishes.*

Avocado Salsa

This is a tangy green salsa made smooth and silky by the addition of avocados. You can use it on tacos or in enchiladas, but you just might find yourself eating it straight with a spoon. Be sure to use soft, ripe avocados.

Yields 4 cups

6 tomatillos, husked and washed, coarsely chopped

2 jalapeños, coarsely chopped

3 garlic cloves

3 medium-size ripe avocados, peeled, pitted, and thinly sliced

5 sprigs cilantro

1 teaspoon salt

1½ cups Mexican crema (or crème fraîche or sour cream)

1. Combine the tomatillos, jalapeños, and garlic in a saucepan, along with a bit of water. Bring to a boil, then reduce heat and simmer for 10 minutes. Remove from heat and let cool a bit.

2. Place the mixture, along with avocados, cilantro, and salt in a food processor or blender. Blend until smooth. Add a little water if necessary to loosen mixture from blender blades.

3. Pour into a bowl and stir in the crema, crème fraîche, or sour cream.

🌶 MEXICAN CREMA

Mexican crema, a cultured cream that many people make at home, is similar to sour cream, but not the same. Crema is less thick and less sour, with just a bit of sweetness. It is also more heat stable than sour cream, though you could easily interchange the two in cooking.

Super Spicy Salsa

You can use salsa in so many ways. It's wonderful in frittatas and delicious as a garnish for chili.

1. In large bowl, combine jalapeños, habanero pepper, bell pepper, garlic, red onion, and tomatoes.

2. In small bowl, combine lemon juice, salt, and pepper; stir to dissolve salt. Add to tomato mixture along with cilantro.

3. Cover and refrigerate for 3–4 hours before serving.

Yields ¼ cup

2 jalapeño peppers, minced
1 habanero pepper, minced
1 green bell pepper, minced
4 cloves garlic, minced
1 red onion, chopped
5 ripe tomatoes, chopped
3 tablespoons lemon juice
¼ teaspoon salt
⅛ teaspoon white pepper
¼ cup chopped fresh cilantro

Zesty Black Bean Salsa

This hearty, filling salsa gets its body from fiber-rich black beans.

Serves 10

1 cup red onion
¼ cup cilantro
¼ cup parsley
1 jalapeño pepper
1½ cups black beans, cooked
4 cups tomatoes, chopped
3 tablespoons lime juice
2 tablespoons olive oil
Freshly ground black pepper

1. Place onion, cilantro, parsley, and jalapeño in food processor; finely chop.

2. In medium bowl, combine onion mixture, black beans, and tomatoes.

3. In separate small bowl, whisk together lime juice, olive oil, and fresh ground pepper. Pour over beans; mix well. Chill before serving.

🌶 USING CANNED BEANS VERSUS COOKING YOUR OWN

Canned beans are very convenient and can save you time. Keep in mind sodium content of recipes will be higher with canned beans. Reduce sodium content in canned beans by draining and thoroughly rinsing with cold water before using.

Black Bean Salsa

This slow cooker recipe makes a lot of salsa, so it's great for parties or large gatherings.

Serves 8

1 (16-ounce) bag dried black beans
Enough water to cover beans by 1"
4 teaspoons salt
2 (15-ounce) cans tomatoes, drained
1 cup corn
1 onion, diced
1 jalapeño, minced
3 cloves garlic, minced
3 teaspoons apple cider vinegar
2 teaspoons sugar
¼ teaspoon black pepper
¼ cup cilantro, chopped

1. Rinse the black beans, then soak overnight. Drain the water and rinse the beans again.

2. In a large pot, add the beans and cover with water. Boil on high heat for 10 minutes, then drain.

3. Add the black beans, water, and 2 teaspoons salt to a 4-quart slow cooker. Cover and cook on high heat for about 5–6 hours. Check the beans at about 5 hours and continue cooking if necessary.

4. Once the beans are done, drain in a colander and allow to cool to room temperature.

5. In a large bowl, combine the beans with the rest of the ingredients.

Homemade Chili Powder

Of course you can go to any store and buy chili powder in a bottle, but where's the fun in that? Making your own is easy and, best of all, you can customize it however you like. Here's a basic recipe, but feel free to tinker with it and add more heat or use different types of chilies.

Yields 1 cup

4 ancho chilies, stemmed, seeded, and roughly chopped
4–5 chiles de árbol, stemmed and seeded
2 tablespoons ground cumin
2 tablespoons garlic powder
1 tablespoon dried oregano
1 teaspoon paprika (hot or sweet)
½ teaspoon cayenne pepper

1. Lightly toast the chilies on a comal or cast-iron skillet until they puff slightly.

2. Put chilies in a food processor or blender and blend until they form a fine powder. Transfer to a bowl.

3. Add the remaining ingredients and stir well until thoroughly mixed.

4. Store in an airtight container for up to 6 months.

🌶 ORIGINS OF CHILI POWDER

No one knows the exact origins of chili powder, but the original version of what you see in supermarkets was created in the United States sometime in the nineteenth century. Chili powder was developed as the way to flavor southwestern staple chili con carne. For every household that made chili, there was likely a unique chili powder blend.

Berbere

This complex, heady spice mix is the foundation for all Ethiopian cooking. There are a lot of ingredients, but it's well worth all the grinding and mixing. Try to use whole spices as much as possible and feel free to adjust seasoning to your liking.

1. Grind all the whole spices in a spice or coffee grinder. Be careful not to inhale all the bits of spice that will be released during the process.

2. Pour all the spices into a bowl and stir well until completely combined.

3. Store in an airtight container in the refrigerator for up to 3 months.

Yields 1 cup

1 teaspoon fenugreek seeds
½ cup dried red chilies such as japones or chiles de árbol, ground
½ cup hot paprika
2 tablespoons salt
1 teaspoon ground ginger
2 teaspoons onion powder
1 teaspoon ground green cardamom
1 teaspoon ground nutmeg
1 teaspoon garlic powder
¼ teaspoon ground cloves
½ teaspoon ground cinnamon
¼ teaspoon ground allspice

🔥 BERBERE

In Ethiopia, the process of making berbere can take days—even up to 1 week. Chilies are often dried in the sun for multiple days, then ground by hand with a mortar and pestle. Then the chilies are combined with other spices and left to dry in the sun again. While the fundamental flavors are the same, families each have their own unique berbere recipe and mix.

Creole Seasoning Blend

The building block for so many great southern dishes like gumbo and jambalaya, this spice blend also works great as a rub for barbecued veggies.

Yields about 1 cup

5 tablespoons hot paprika
3 tablespoons kosher salt
2 tablespoons garlic powder
2 tablespoons onion powder
2 tablespoons dried oregano
2 tablespoons dried basil
2 tablespoons black pepper
1 tablespoon dried thyme
1 tablespoon cayenne pepper
1 tablespoon white pepper

1. Combine all ingredients in a bowl and stir well.

2. Store in an airtight container for up to 6 months.

Adobo Seasoning

Adobo is a spice mixture that is used throughout Latin America and the Caribbean. Try it on veggies— then grill, roast, or fry.

1. Put all ingredients in a bowl and stir until thoroughly combined.

2. Store in an airtight container for up to a year.

Yields 1½ cups

6 tablespoons kosher salt
6 tablespoons granulated garlic
2 tablespoons ground black pepper
2 tablespoons onion powder
2 tablespoons ground cumin
2 tablespoons ground coriander
2 tablespoons chili powder (a smoky, chipotle powder would be good, but use whatever you have on hand)
¼ teaspoon allspice
½ teaspoon dried oregano

Curry Powder

This basic curry powder recipe, which you should take and customize to your own liking, will give you a new appreciation for this complex spice mix that adds flavor to so many dishes. Use ground spices or grind your own.

Yields 1 cup

6 tablespoons ground coriander
4 tablespoons ground cumin
2 tablespoons black pepper
2 tablespoons ground cinnamon
1 tablespoon turmeric
1 tablespoon ground ginger
1 tablespoon cayenne pepper
1 teaspoon ground nutmeg
1 teaspoon ground cloves

1. Grind whatever spices need grinding.

2. Combine all ingredients and stir until well combined.

3. Store in an airtight container for up to 6 months.

🔥 TURMERIC

Turmeric is the spice that gives all curry powder its distinct yellow-orange hue. Turmeric has an astringent yet earthy flavor, akin to mustard or horseradish, but more mellow. Its strong color will dye any food that it is sprinkled on. You might also find fresh turmeric at specialty grocery stores, where it looks similar to its cousin, ginger.

Ras El Hanout

The Arabic phrase *ras el hanout* means "top of the shop" and refers to a spice owner's special blend of his best spices. It's an essential Moroccan spice mix and some versions have upward of twenty or even thirty ingredients.

1. Combine all the spices and stir until thoroughly mixed.

2. Store in an airtight container for up to 6 months.

Yields ¼ cup

1 teaspoon ground cloves
1 teaspoon ground ginger
1 teaspoon ground cardamom
1 teaspoon ground mace
1 teaspoon ground nutmeg
1 teaspoon ground black pepper
1 teaspoon ground cinnamon
1 teaspoon ground allspice
1 teaspoon ground turmeric
1 teaspoon hot paprika

Baharat

Baharat is a spice mix used throughout the Middle East: Lebanon, Syria, Israel, Jordan. Its name simply means "spice" in Arabic. There are endless variations, so feel free to experiment. Try Baharat on different vegetables, or stirred into rice pilaf.

Yields ½ cup

2 tablespoons ground black peppercorns
2 tablespoons hot paprika
1 tablespoon ground coriander seeds
1 tablespoon ground cumin
1 tablespoon ground cloves
1 tablespoon ground mint
2 teaspoons ground nutmeg
1 teaspoon ground cinnamon

1. Combine all spices and mix well.

2. Store in an airtight container for up to 6 months.

CHAPTER 5

Soups, Stews, and Chilies

Vegetable Stock

Red Lentil Soup

Curried Red Lentil Soup

Hot and Sour Soup

Tortilla Soup

Jamaican Red Bean Stew

Chilled Curry Potato-Fennel Soup

Dahl

Ethiopian Lentil Stew

Curried Seitan Stew

Posole

Korean-Style Hot Pot

Vegan Chili

Southwest Vegetable Chili

Five-Pepper Chili

Fajita Chili

Acorn Squash Chili

Summer Chili

Tabasco Gazpacho

Tortilla Stew

Vegetable Stock

Other veggies, such as fennel, ginger, parsnips, herbs, and so on, may be substituted for any of the ingredients. This is a very changeable recipe, open to personalization, that will act as the base for many of the recipes in this chapter and elsewhere in this book.

Yields about 4 cups

1 onion, sliced

1 leek, white part only, cleaned thoroughly and sliced

1 carrot, peeled and sliced

2 stalks celery, roughly chopped

1 turnip, peeled and sliced

5 cloves garlic, peeled and sliced

6 cups cold water

Small bunch of parsley stems

10 black peppercorns

8 sprigs fresh thyme

1 bay leaf

Salt and pepper (optional)

Combine all ingredients in a large stockpot. Simmer 1 hour; strain. Season with salt and pepper if desired; cool. Keeps refrigerated for 1 week. Freezes well.

Red Lentil Soup

This hearty, spicy, slow cooker dish can act as a side or a meal. But whenever you choose to serve this soup, you'll be blown away by the spicy flavors that make the tip of your tongue tingle.

1. Rinse the lentils carefully and sort through the bunch to remove any dirt or debris.

2. In a sauté pan, heat the olive oil over medium heat, then sauté the onion, ginger, and garlic for 2–3 minutes.

3. In a 4-quart slow cooker, add the sautéed vegetables and all remaining ingredients. Cover and cook on low for 6–8 hours. Add more salt, if necessary, to taste.

Serves 6

2 cups red lentils
3 tablespoons olive oil
1 small onion, sliced
1½ teaspoons fresh ginger, peeled and minced
2 cloves garlic, minced
6 cups Vegetable Stock (see recipe in this chapter)
Juice of 1 lemon
½ teaspoon paprika
1 teaspoon cayenne pepper
1½ teaspoons salt

Curried Red Lentil Soup

This simple, hearty soup can be made as spicy as you like. For a different dimension of spice, chop up fresh cilantro or parsley and use them as a garnish.

Serves 4

2 tablespoons butter
1 large onion, finely chopped
2 carrots, finely chopped
2 cups red lentils, picked through for stones
½ teaspoon hot paprika
½ teaspoon red pepper flakes
½ teaspoon cumin
4 cups Vegetable Stock (see recipe in this chapter)
2 tablespoons lemon juice
Salt and pepper, to taste
Handful of chopped fresh jalapeños or serranos, for garnish

1. Melt the butter in the bottom of a pot. Add the onion and carrots and sauté until they are softened, about 3–4 minutes.

2. Add the lentils and spices and stir, making sure all the lentils are coated.

3. Add the Vegetable Stock. Bring to a boil, then lower the heat and let simmer for 20 minutes or until the lentils are soft. Add the lemon juice and stir. Taste and season with salt and pepper.

4. If you like, you can purée the soup in a blender or with a handheld blender. If you like a chunkier soup, skip blending.

5. Serve in bowls, garnished with jalapeños or serranos.

🌶 WHAT ARE LENTILS?

Lentils, like beans and peas, are legumes, types of flowering plants that have been cultivated since ancient Egypt. Lentils themselves are the edible seeds of the plant and they come in a wide variety of colors and sizes. Red lentils, which cook down to a more yellow color, are among the most common, along with brown and yellow. There are also small, deep green French Le Puy lentils, which have earned the nickname "poor man's caviar."

Hot and Sour Soup

Adjust the spiciness of this slow cooker soup by adding more or less chili paste, to taste.

1. In a 4-quart slow cooker, add all ingredients except for the cornstarch mixture; cook on low for 6 hours.

2. Pour in the cornstarch mixture; stir, and cook on high heat for 20 additional minutes.

Serves 6

4 cups Vegetable Stock (see recipe in this chapter)
2 tablespoons soy sauce
2 tablespoons rice vinegar
1 teaspoon sesame oil
2 ounces dried Chinese mushrooms
½ cup canned bamboo shoots, sliced
4 ounces extra-firm tofu, cubed
1 tablespoon red chili paste
1 teaspoon white pepper
2 tablespoons cornstarch mixed with ¼ cup water

Tortilla Soup

Turn this slow cooker soup into a complete meal by adding pieces of cooked vegetarian chicken, such as Morningstar Farms Meal Starters Chik'n Strips or Gardein Seasoned Bites.

Serves 8

2 tablespoons olive oil
1 large onion, chopped
2 cloves garlic, minced
2 tablespoons soy sauce
7 cups Vegetable Stock (see recipe in this chapter)
12 ounces firm silken tofu, crumbled
2 cups tomato, diced
1 cup corn kernels
1 teaspoon chipotle powder
1 teaspoon cayenne pepper
2 teaspoons ground cumin
2 teaspoons salt
1 teaspoon dried oregano
10 small corn tortillas, sliced
8 ounces shredded Monterey jack cheese or vegan cheese, such as Daiya Mozzarella Style Shreds

1. In a sauté pan over medium heat, add the olive oil; sauté the onion until just soft, about 3 minutes. Add the garlic and sauté for an additional 30 seconds.

2. In a 4-quart slow cooker, add all ingredients except tortillas and cheese. Stir, cover, and cook over low heat for 4 hours.

3. While the soup is cooking, preheat oven to 450°F. Slice the corn tortillas into thin strips and place them on an ungreased baking sheet. Bake for about 10 minutes, or until they turn golden brown. Remove from heat and set aside.

4. After the soup has cooled slightly, use an immersion blender or regular blender to purée the soup.

5. Serve with cooked tortilla strips and 1 ounce of shredded cheese in each bowl of soup.

🌶 CHIPOTLE POWDER

Chipotle powder is made from ground chipotle peppers, a type of dried jalapeño. They bring a smoky spiciness to dishes, but can be replaced with cayenne pepper or chili powder.

Jamaican Red Bean Stew

Make your own jerk seasoning to pump up the taste of this spicy, slow cooker recipe by combining thyme, allspice, black pepper, cinnamon, cayenne, onion powder, and nutmeg.

1. In a sauté pan over medium heat, add the olive oil, then sauté the onion and garlic for about 3 minutes.

2. In a 4-quart slow cooker, add all ingredients. Cover and cook on low heat for 6 hours.

Serves 4

2 tablespoons olive oil
½ onion, diced
2 garlic cloves, minced
1 (15-ounce) can diced tomatoes
3 cups sweet potatoes, peeled and diced
2 (15-ounce) cans red kidney beans, drained
1 cup coconut milk
3 cups Vegetable Stock (see recipe in this chapter)
2 teaspoons jerk seasoning
2 teaspoons curry powder
Salt and pepper, to taste

Chilled Curry Potato-Fennel Soup

While this soup is delicious hot or cold, it's particularly refreshing in the summer, with enough substance to stand on its own as a main course.

Serves 10–12

1 large Idaho russet potato, peeled
1 large Spanish onion, peeled
1 head sweet fennel, tassel-like fronds removed and set aside
1 red bell pepper
1 tablespoon olive oil
1 (1") piece of fresh ginger, peeled and finely chopped
2 cloves garlic, peeled and finely chopped
2 teaspoons good-quality Madras curry powder
3 cups Vegetable Stock (see recipe in this chapter)
1 jalapeño pepper, seeded and finely chopped
1 quart buttermilk
1 cup half-and-half
Salt and white pepper, to taste
1 tablespoon chopped Italian parsley

1. Chop the potato, onion, fennel, and red bell pepper coarsely. In a large soup pot over medium-high heat, heat the oil for 1 minute. Add the chopped vegetables, ginger, and garlic. Cook until onion is translucent, about 5 minutes; stir in curry powder and cook 5 minutes more. Add Vegetable Stock; raise heat to high and bring to a full boil. Reduce to a simmer; cook until potatoes are falling-apart tender, about 15 minutes.

2. Chill and purée the soup in a blender or food processor. Add the chopped jalapeño, buttermilk, and half-and-half. Season to taste with salt and white pepper. Serve garnished with chopped parsley and/or sprigs from the reserved fennel fronds.

Dahl

A hearty dish that will have your kitchen nice and fragrant. Serve with rice and garnish with chopped fresh chilies for extra spice.

1. Cook the lentils. Place them in a large pot and cover them with salted water. Bring to a boil, then reduce heat and let simmer until tender, about 20 minutes.

2. Drain lentils, but reserve their cooking water.

3. In a skillet over medium-high heat, heat the oil or butter. Add the mustard seeds and cook until they begin to dance around in the pan.

4. Add ginger, garlic, onions, and serrano peppers. Sauté until the onions and garlic are golden brown, about 5 minutes.

5. Add coriander and cumin and stir. Add chopped tomatoes. Sauté mixture until the tomatoes are softened and well cooked, 6–8 minutes.

6. Add 1 cup reserved lentil cooking water to skillet, bring to boil and lower heat. Add cooked lentils and stir to combine. Add salt and pepper, to taste, and let simmer another few minutes over low heat.

7. Just before you are ready to serve the Dahl, take off heat and add cilantro leaves.

Serves 4

1 cup red lentils
2 tablespoons vegetable oil or butter
1 teaspoon mustard seeds
2 tablespoons fresh ginger, peeled and finely chopped
5 cloves of garlic, peeled and finely minced
2 onions, roughly chopped
3 serrano peppers, seeded and finely minced
1 tablespoon ground coriander
1 tablespoon ground cumin
4 tomatoes, seeded and roughly chopped
Salt and pepper, to taste
2 tablespoons fresh cilantro leaves, finely chopped

Ethiopian Lentil Stew

The Ethiopian spice mix Berbere (see Chapter 4) can make anything taste extraordinary, even a humble stew of lentils. Sprinkle some raw, chopped jalapeños on top for extra heat.

Serves 6

2 cups red lentils
½ cup olive oil
1 red onion, finely chopped
2 garlic cloves, peeled and minced
1 tablespoon finely chopped jalapeño peppers
4 tomatoes, roughly chopped
Juice of 1 lemon
3 teaspoons Berbere (see Chapter 4)
1 tablespoon fresh parsley, minced
Salt, to taste

1. Put lentils in large pot and cover by at least 2" with salted water. Bring to a boil, then reduce heat and let simmer until tender, about 15–20 minutes. Drain well and set aside.

2. Heat olive oil in a large skillet or sauté pan. Add the onion, garlic, and jalapeños and sauté until the onion is soft and translucent, about 5 minutes.

3. Add the lentils, tomatoes, lemon juice, Berbere, parsley, and salt. Stir to combine.

4. Cook mixture on low heat until everything is heated through, about 3–4 minutes.

Curried Seitan Stew

Adding a small amount of soy sauce to a curry dish gives it a richness that is normally achieved with fish sauce in recipes that aren't vegetarian. That richness carries over to the hot ingredients in this slow cooker dish and you'll really be able to taste the spice!

1. In a 4-quart slow cooker, add all ingredients except for the cilantro. Cover and cook on low heat for 4 hours.

2. Garnish with cilantro before serving.

Serves 4

2 tablespoons olive oil
½ onion, chopped
2 cloves garlic, minced
1 teaspoon fresh ginger, minced
2 tablespoons panang curry paste
1 teaspoon paprika
1 teaspoon sugar
½ teaspoon cayenne pepper
1 teaspoon soy sauce
1 (14-ounce) can coconut milk
3 cups Vegetable Stock (see recipe in this chapter)
2 cups seitan, cubed
½ teaspoon salt
¼ teaspoon pepper
¼ cup cilantro, chopped

Posole

This spicy, slow cooker stew just needs a sprinkling of shredded red cabbage to finish it to perfection.

Serves 6

8 large dried New Mexican red chilies
1½ quarts Vegetable Stock (see recipe in this chapter)
3 cloves garlic, minced
2 tablespoons lime juice
1 tablespoon ground cumin
1 tablespoon oregano
1 (7-ounce) package Gardein Chick'n Strips
¾ cup flour
1 teaspoon canola oil
1 large onion, sliced
40 ounces canned hominy

1. Seed the chilies, reserving the seeds.

2. In a dry, hot frying pan, heat the chilies until warmed through and fragrant, about 2–3 minutes. Do not burn or brown them.

3. In a medium pot, place the chilies and seeds, 1 quart Vegetable Stock, garlic, lime juice, cumin, and oregano. Bring to a boil and continue to boil for 20 minutes.

4. Meanwhile, in a plastic bag, toss the Chick'n Strips with the flour to coat. Heat the oil in a large nonstick skillet and brown the vegan meat on all sides, about 3 minutes.

5. Add the onion and cook about 5 minutes, or until the onion is soft.

6. In a 4-quart slow cooker, pour the unused Vegetable Stock, hominy, and Chick'n and onion mixture.

7. Strain the chili–Vegetable Stock mixture through a mesh sieve into the slow cooker insert, mashing down with a wooden spoon to press out the pulp and juice. Discard the seeds and remaining solids.

8. Cook on low for 8 hours.

Korean-Style Hot Pot

Serve this hot and spicy slow cooker dish with sides of steamed rice and kimchi.

1. Remove the leaves of the baby bok choy. Wash thoroughly.

2. Place the leaves whole in a 4-quart slow cooker. Add the water, cremini mushrooms, tofu, garlic, sesame oil, and crushed red pepper. Stir.

3. Cook on low for 8 hours.

4. Add the enoki mushrooms and stir. Cook an additional 30 minutes.

Serves 8

3 bunches baby bok choy
8 cups water
8 ounces sliced cremini mushrooms
12 ounces extra-firm tofu, cubed
3 cloves garlic, thinly sliced
¼ teaspoon sesame oil
1 tablespoon crushed red pepper flakes
7 ounces enoki mushrooms

Vegan Chili

This hearty warm-up goes especially well with Spicy Southwestern Corn Bread (see Chapter 3) and a tall glass of lemonade.

Serves 8

¼ cup olive oil
2 cups chopped onions
1 cup chopped carrots
2 cups chopped assorted bell peppers
2 teaspoons salt
1 tablespoon chopped garlic
2 chopped, seeded jalapeño peppers
1 tablespoon ground ancho chili pepper or ½ teaspoon crushed red pepper flakes
1 chipotle pepper in adobo, chopped
1 tablespoon toasted cumin seeds, ground, or 4 teaspoons ground cumin, toasted briefly in a dry pan
1 (28-ounce) can plum tomatoes, roughly chopped, juice included
3 (16-ounce) cans beans: 1 each red kidney, cannellini, and black beans, rinsed and drained, or an equal amount of home-cooked beans (start with about 1½ cups dried beans)
1 cup of tomato juice
Finely chopped red onions
Chopped fresh cilantro

1. Heat the oil in a heavy-bottomed Dutch oven or soup pot. Add the onions, carrots, bell peppers, and salt; cook 15 minutes over medium heat, until the onions are soft. Add the garlic, jalapeños, ancho, chipotle, and cumin; cook 5 minutes more.

2. Stir in tomatoes, beans, and tomato juice. Simmer about 45 minutes. Serve garnished with red onions and cilantro.

Southwest Vegetable Chili

Southwestern cuisine is similar to Mexican food and includes a wide variety of peppers, such as the jalapeños, bell peppers, chipotle, and chili powder found in this slow cooker recipe.

In a 4-quart slow cooker, add all ingredients. Cover and cook on low heat for 5 hours.

Serves 4

1 (28-ounce) can diced tomatoes
1 (15-ounce) can red kidney beans
1 onion, chopped
1 green bell pepper, chopped
1 red bell pepper, chopped
1 zucchini, chopped
1 squash, chopped
¼ cup pickled jalapeños, chopped
⅛ cup chili powder
2 tablespoons garlic powder
2 tablespoons cumin
1 teaspoon chipotle powder
⅛ teaspoon dried thyme
1 teaspoon salt
¼ teaspoon black pepper

Five-Pepper Chili

Sound the alarm! This spicy, slow cooker chili will set your mouth aflame.

Serves 8

1 onion, diced
1 jalapeño, seeded and minced
1 habanero pepper, seeded and
  minced
1 bell pepper, diced
1 poblano pepper, seeded and
  diced
2 cloves garlic, minced
2 (15-ounce) cans crushed
  tomatoes
2 cups fresh tomatoes, diced
2 tablespoons chili powder
1 tablespoon cumin
½ tablespoon cayenne pepper
⅛ cup vegan Worcestershire
  sauce
2 (15-ounce) cans pinto beans
1 teaspoon salt
¼ teaspoon black pepper

In a 4-quart slow cooker, add all ingredients. Cover and cook on low heat for 5 hours.

Fajita Chili

Use this slow cooker Fajita Chili to re-create the flavor of sizzling restaurant fajitas in your own home!

In a 4-quart slow cooker, add all ingredients. Cover and cook on low heat for 5 hours.

Serves 6

1 red onion, diced

1 jalapeño, seeded and minced

3 cloves garlic, minced

1 (15-ounce) can black beans, drained

1 (15-ounce) can diced tomatoes, drained

1 (8-ounce) package Morningstar Farms Meal Starters Chik'n Strips, cut into bite-size pieces

2 cups Vegetable Stock (see recipe in this chapter)

2 teaspoons chili powder

1 teaspoon sugar

1 teaspoon paprika

¼ teaspoon garlic powder

¼ teaspoon cayenne pepper

¼ teaspoon cumin

1 teaspoon salt

¼ teaspoon black pepper

Acorn Squash Chili

Acorn squash keeps its shape in this slow cooker chili, giving it a chunky texture to go along with its spicy bite!

Serves 8

2 cups acorn squash, cubed
2 (15-ounce) cans petite diced
  tomatoes
2 stalks celery, diced
1 medium onion, diced
3 cloves garlic, minced
2 carrots, diced
1 teaspoon mesquite liquid
  smoke
2 teaspoons hot sauce
1 teaspoon chili powder
1 teaspoon paprika
1 teaspoon oregano
1 teaspoon smoked paprika
1 (15-ounce) can kidney beans,
  drained and rinsed
1 (15-ounce) can cannellini
  beans, drained and rinsed
1 cup fresh corn kernels

1. In a 4-quart slow cooker, add all ingredients except the corn. Cover and cook for 8 hours on low.

2. Add the corn and stir. Cover and continue to cook on low for 30 minutes. Stir before serving.

Summer Chili

This slow cooker chili is full of spicy summer vegetables like habanero peppers, and you can add vegetarian chicken to make this a heartier dish.

1. In a 4-quart slow cooker, add the fennel, radishes, celery, carrots, onion, shallot, garlic, habanero, beans, tomato paste, and all spices; stir. Cook on low for 6–7 hours.

2. Stir in the zucchinis, tomatoes, and corn. Cook for an additional 30 minutes on high. Stir before serving.

🌶 CAMPARI TOMATOES

Campari is a type of tomato that is grown on the vine and has a sweet, juicy taste. It is round and on the small side, but not as small as a cherry tomato.

Serves 8

1 bulb fennel, diced
4 radishes, diced
2 stalks celery including leaves, diced
2 carrots, cut into coin-size pieces
1 medium onion, diced
1 shallot, diced
4 cloves garlic, sliced
1 habanero pepper, diced
1 (15-ounce) can cannellini beans, drained and rinsed
1 (12-ounce) can tomato paste
½ teaspoon dried oregano
½ teaspoon black pepper
½ teaspoon crushed rosemary
½ teaspoon cayenne
½ teaspoon ground chipotle
1 teaspoon chili powder
1 teaspoon tarragon
¼ teaspoon cumin
¼ teaspoon celery seed
2 zucchinis, cubed
10 campari tomatoes, quartered
1 cup corn kernels

Tabasco Gazpacho

By roasting the tomatoes and red peppers first, this cold soup gets an even richer, more concentrated flavor. Using the best quality olive oil you have on hand makes it even better.

Serves 4–6

2 pounds tomatoes
2 red bell peppers
1 big chunk of day-old French bread, crust removed
2 cucumbers, peeled, seeded, and chopped
4 garlic cloves, peeled and finely minced
2 tablespoons sherry vinegar
1–2 tablespoons Tabasco, to taste
½ cup olive oil
1 teaspoon fresh tarragon, minced (or a pinch of dried tarragon)
Salt and black pepper, to taste

1. Heat the oven to 350°F. Put the tomatoes and bell peppers in a baking pan and roast for 30–40 minutes, until they are softened and the peppers are lightly charred. Remove from oven.

2. Transfer roasted vegetables to a large bowl and let sit, covered, for 20–30 minutes to cool.

3. Cut or tear bread into 1" pieces. Soak the bread in a small bowl of water for 10–15 minutes.

4. When vegetables are cool enough to handle, remove peels, stems, and seeds. Do this over a bowl to make sure to catch their juices. Tear the tomatoes and peppers apart into small pieces and return to large bowl. Strain the juices and add to the tomato and pepper mixture.

5. Add cucumbers, garlic, vinegar, Tabasco, and olive oil to bowl.

6. Remove bread from soaking liquid. Do not squeeze out excess liquid. Add bread to bowl, along with tarragon, salt, and pepper.

7. Transfer all ingredients to blender and blend until smooth. The soup should be smooth but with a slightly rough texture.

8. Place soup in a serving bowl and refrigerate for at least 3 hours before serving.

HOT HANDS!

If you think your job is sometimes painful, try picking chili peppers for a living. Hot hands is a commonly reported ailment among Tabasco chili pickers. Tabascos must be picked when they are ripe, which means they are more likely to break, which in turn releases a flood of capsaicin over workers' hands. Many Tabasco pickers suffer from hands that constantly tingle with a bit of pain and heat.

Tortilla Stew

These softened tortilla chips are perfect for brunch because they only take a few minutes to throw together once the ingredients are assembled.

Serves 2

4 cups tortilla chips (any color)
2 cups Vegetable Stock (see recipe in this chapter)
1 cup New Mexico Chili Sauce (see Chapter 2) or spicy tomato sauce
4 large eggs (optional)
2 tablespoons sour cream
Chopped cilantro

Place the chips in a large skillet over a high flame. Add 1 cup of Vegetable Stock and the New Mexico Chili Sauce or spicy tomato sauce. Bring to a boil, then lower to a simmer, adding more Vegetable Stock as needed to keep the mixture soupy. Cook until the tortillas are well softened, but not mushy. If using, fry the eggs in a little butter. Serve the Tortilla Stew on 2 plates, topped with fried eggs if desired, a dollop of sour cream, and a sprinkling of chopped cilantro.

CHAPTER 6

Grains, Beans, and Legumes

New Orleans Red Beans and Rice

Kimchi Fried Rice

Rice Cooked with Ancho Chili

Spicy Green Rice

Chipotle-Thyme Black Beans

Creole Jambalaya

Spanish Rice

Curried Rice

Thai Green Curry Tofu

Curried Lentils

Red Lentil Curry

Curried Parsnips

Black Bean–Cilantro Fritters

Chana Masala

Spicy Black-Eyed Peas and Kale

Red Bean Fritters

Chickpeas in Potato-Onion Curry

Curried Green Beans

New Orleans Red Beans and Rice

This spicy, slow cooker dish is a New Orleans staple that is traditionally served on Mondays.

Serves 8

¼ cup butter or vegan margarine
1 cup onion, diced
1 cup green bell pepper, diced
1 cup celery, diced
5 cloves garlic, minced
2 (15-ounce) cans red kidney beans, drained
1½ cups water
4 teaspoons salt
2 teaspoons liquid smoke
1 teaspoon vegan Worcestershire sauce
2 teaspoons hot sauce
1 teaspoon dried thyme
2 teaspoons cayenne pepper
4 bay leaves
8 cups cooked long-grain white rice

1. Add the butter or vegan margarine to a 4-quart slow cooker and sauté the onion, green bell pepper, celery, and garlic for 3–5 minutes over high heat.

2. Add the red kidney beans, water, salt, liquid smoke, Worcestershire sauce, hot sauce, dried thyme, cayenne pepper, and bay leaves. Cover and cook on low heat for about 6 hours.

3. Remove the bay leaves and serve over the cooked white rice.

🔥 MAKE IT "MEATY"

Sausage and ham hocks are the most common meats used in red beans and rice. To make a vegetarian "meaty" version, add cooked, sliced vegetarian sausage and chunks of cooked vegetarian bacon right before serving.

Kimchi Fried Rice

This is great way to use up old rice. It's also a good introduction to using kimchi—the strong flavor might take a bit of getting used to. Make sure your fried eggs have a runny yolk, which will help form a sauce of sorts.

1. Over medium-high heat, heat oil in a large skillet. Add kimchi and fry until it is heated through, about 4 minutes.

2. Add gochujang and stir to combine.

3. Add rice. Use a wooden spoon or spatula to break up the rice and stir well to ensure it is well coated and mixed with kimchi and pepper paste. You might want to add just a little bit of water to help loosen the rice up.

4. Add sesame oil and stir. Add salt and pepper. Taste rice and adjust seasoning as you like.

5. Turn heat to low and cover while you fry your eggs.

6. After eggs are fried, divide rice evenly into 4 bowls. Top with fried eggs and a sprinkling of scallions.

Serves 4

2 tablespoons vegetable oil
4 cups kimchi, cut into bite-size pieces
1 tablespoon gochujang
4–5 cups cold rice
1 tablespoon sesame oil
Salt and pepper, to taste
4 fried eggs
Handful scallions, finely chopped, for garnish

Rice Cooked with Ancho Chili

Try this as a mild but still spicy side dish for grilled or roasted veggies.

Serves 4

¾ cup long-grain white rice
2 ancho chilies, seeds and ribs removed
1 cup water or Vegetable Stock (see Chapter 5)
3 tablespoons vegetable oil
¼ cup finely chopped white onion
Salt, to taste

1. Put the rice in a bowl and cover with hot water for 5 minutes. Rinse well and set aside to drain.

2. Lightly toast the anchos on a comal or cast-iron skillet for a few seconds on each side. (Be careful not to burn them or they will get bitter.) Put in a bowl and cover with hot water or Vegetable Stock and let soak until softened, about 15 minutes. Remove from water and cut into thin strips. Save the soaking liquid.

3. Heat the oil in a heavy-bottomed saucepan or deep skillet. Add the dry rice and stir until all the grains have been coated in a bit of oil. Add the onion and continue frying over medium heat until the rice starts to brown lightly, about 5 minutes.

4. Add the water or Vegetable Stock, ancho chilies, salt, and ½ cup of the soaking liquid to the rice. Cook, covered, on low heat until all the liquid has been absorbed, about 12–15 minutes.

5. Take off heat, set aside, and leave covered for a few minutes. Give the rice a stir to fluff it up before serving.

Spicy Green Rice

A nice way to introduce a bit of spice into a meal is through a side dish like this Spicy Green Rice.

1. Cover the rice with hot water and let soak for 5 minutes. Rinse well and set to drain.

2. Heat the oil in a heavy-bottomed saucepan or deep skillet. Add the dry rice and stir until all the grains have been coated in a bit of oil. Add the onion and 1 clove of garlic and continue frying over medium heat until the rice starts to brown lightly, about 5 minutes.

3. Purée the chilies, tomatillos, and other garlic clove with ¼ cup of the Vegetable Stock in a blender. Stir the mixture into the rice and fry for a few minutes more, stirring to prevent burning, until the moisture has been mostly absorbed.

4. Add the remaining Vegetable Stock, salt, and cilantro and cook over medium heat until all the liquid has been absorbed, about 12–15 minutes.

5. Take off heat, set aside, and leave covered for a few minutes. Give the rice a stir to fluff it up before serving.

Serves 6

1 cup long-grain rice
¼ cup vegetable oil
½ white onion, roughly chopped
2 garlic cloves, peeled and roughly chopped
4 jalapeño peppers
4 tomatillos
1¼ cups Vegetable Stock (see Chapter 5), separated
Salt, to taste
4 cilantro leaves, finely chopped

Chipotle-Thyme Black Beans

The chipotle in this spicy, pressure cooker recipe will knock your socks off! Possibly the most famous dried chili outside of Mexico, chipotles are simply red, ripened jalapeños that are smoked and dried.

Serves 8

2 cups dried black beans
16 cups water
1 tablespoon vegetable oil
1 teaspoon chipotle powder
2 teaspoons fresh thyme, minced
1 teaspoon salt

1. Add the beans and 8 cups water to the pressure cooker. Lock the lid into place; bring to high pressure for 1 minute. Remove from heat and quick-release the pressure.

2. Drain the water, rinse the beans, and add to the pressure cooker again with the remaining 8 cups water. Let soak for 1 hour.

3. Add the vegetable oil, chipotle, thyme, and salt. Lock the lid into place; bring to high pressure and maintain for 12 minutes. Remove from heat and allow pressure to release naturally.

Creole Jambalaya

Try Morningstar Farms Meal Starters Chik'n Strips and Tofurky Andouille Sausages as an alternative to real meat in this hot and spicy, pressure cooker recipe.

1. Melt the butter or margarine in the pressure cooker over medium-low heat, then add the onion, bell pepper, celery, and garlic. Cook for about 15 minutes, until soft.

2. Add the Vegetable Stock, water, tomato sauce, rice, bay leaves, thyme, cayenne, and Cajun seasoning, then stir.

3. Lock the lid into place; bring to high pressure and maintain for 6 minutes. Remove from heat and allow pressure to release naturally.

4. Stir in prepared chopped vegetarian chicken and sausage, if using, and let stand for 5 minutes. Season with salt, to taste.

Serves 8

½ cup butter or vegan margarine, such as Earth Balance
1 cup onion, chopped
1 medium bell pepper, chopped
2 stalks celery, chopped
3 cloves garlic, minced
3 cups Vegetable Stock (see Chapter 5)
1 cup water
8 ounces tomato sauce
2 cups white rice
2 bay leaves
2 teaspoons thyme
2 teaspoons cayenne
2 teaspoons Cajun seasoning
2 cups cooked vegetarian chicken and sausage (optional)
Salt, to taste

🔥 CREOLE CUISINE

Creole cuisine is similar to, but more refined than, Cajun cooking, and both use the Holy Trinity of onion, bell pepper, and celery as the base of many dishes. It hails from southern Louisiana, but is influenced by Spanish, French, and African cuisines.

Spanish Rice

Cooking rice in tomatoes, chili powder, and bell pepper is the key to this slow cooker Spanish Rice.

Serves 8

2 cups white rice, uncooked
2 tablespoons butter or vegan margarine
2 cups water
2 cups Vegetable Stock (see Chapter 5)
1 onion, diced
1 green bell pepper, diced
1 cup canned tomatoes, diced
⅛ cup pickled jalapeños, diced
1 teaspoon chili powder
½ teaspoon garlic powder
1 teaspoon salt
¼ teaspoon black pepper

Add all ingredients to a 4-quart slow cooker. Cover and cook on low heat for 4–5 hours.

Curried Rice

This slow cooker Curried Rice is a great side dish for a spicy meal!

1. Add all the ingredients to a 4-quart slow cooker except the lime juice and cilantro.

2. Cover and cook on low heat for 4–5 hours.

3. Stir in the lime juice and cilantro and cook for 30 more minutes before serving.

Serves 4

2 cups white rice, uncooked
2 tablespoons olive oil
2 cups water
2 cups Vegetable Stock (see Chapter 5)
2 tablespoons Curry Powder (see Chapter 4)
1 teaspoon salt
¼ teaspoon black pepper
1 tablespoon lime juice
¼ cup cilantro, chopped

Thai Green Curry Tofu

Use this recipe as a guideline, adding or using different vegetables according to your own preference, and using as much or as little Green Curry Paste as you like. Serve with white or brown rice.

Serves 4–6

2 tablespoons vegetable oil
½ onion, chopped
4 tablespoons Green Curry
    Paste (see Chapter 2)
1 (15-ounce) can coconut milk
1 (16-ounce) package firm tofu,
    drained and cut into cubes
2 carrots, sliced
1 red bell pepper, seeded and
    cut into chunks
1 cup snow peas
Handful fresh basil leaves,
    roughly chopped
Handful fresh cilantro leaves,
    roughly chopped

1. Heat oil in a wok or large, deep-frying pan over medium-high heat. Add onion and sauté 1–2 minutes. Add Green Curry Paste and stir-fry until fragrant, about 2–3 minutes.

2. Add the coconut milk and stir until ingredients come together. Add the tofu and stir to combine. Cover and let simmer for 5 minutes.

3. Add carrots, bell pepper, and snow peas. Stir and cook 3–5 minutes, until vegetables are cooked through but still firm and crisp.

4. Transfer to serving bowl and sprinkle with fresh basil and cilantro.

Curried Lentils

Serve this Indian-style, slow cooker dish with hot rice or naan, an Indian flatbread. It can also be served with plain yogurt or vegan yogurt to cut heat.

1. Heat the butter or oil in a nonstick pan. Sauté the onion slices until they start to brown, about 8–10 minutes.

2. Add the garlic, jalapeños, red pepper flakes, and cumin. Sauté for 2–3 minutes.

3. Add the onion mixture to a 4-quart slow cooker.

4. Sort through the lentils and discard any rocks or foreign matter. Add the lentils to the slow cooker. Stir in the water, salt, and turmeric.

5. Cover and cook on high for 2½ hours.

6. Add the spinach and stir. Cook on high for an additional 15 minutes.

Serves 6

2 teaspoons butter or canola oil
1 large onion, thinly sliced
2 cloves garlic, minced
2 jalapeños, diced
½ teaspoon red pepper flakes
½ teaspoon ground cumin
1 pound yellow lentils
6 cups water
½ teaspoon salt
½ teaspoon ground turmeric
4 cups chopped fresh spinach

Red Lentil Curry

You can simplify the spicy seasoning in this pressure cooker dish by omitting the turmeric and ginger.

Serves 8

2 cups dried red lentils
8 cups water
3 tablespoons olive oil
1 teaspoon salt, plus more to taste
1 cup onion, diced
1 teaspoon garlic, minced
1 teaspoon fresh ginger, peeled and minced
3 tablespoons curry powder
1 teaspoon turmeric
1 teaspoon cumin
1 teaspoon chili powder
1 teaspoon sugar
1 (6-ounce) can tomato paste
Pepper, to taste

1. Add the lentils, water, 1 tablespoon oil, and 1 teaspoon salt to the pressure cooker.

2. Lock the lid into place; bring to high pressure and maintain for 7 minutes. Remove from heat and allow pressure to release naturally.

3. In a pan, add the remaining oil and sauté the onion until it is caramelized. Add the garlic and ginger and sauté for 1 minute more. Add the curry powder, turmeric, cumin, chili powder, sugar, and tomato paste, and bring the mixture to a simmer for 2–3 minutes, stirring constantly.

4. Drain the lentils and add to the curry mixture. Taste for seasoning and add salt and pepper, to taste.

Curried Parsnips

The herby sweetness of parsnips lends itself well to curries. Try this one over brown rice with a little lentil dahl for a delicious dinner that's a complete protein dish to boot!

Boil the parsnips until halfway done, about 5 minutes; drain. Melt the butter or heat the oil in a large, heavy-bottomed skillet. Add the onion, pears or apples, curry, and coriander and cook over medium flame, stirring regularly until onion is soft, about 10 minutes. Add the parsnips, season well with salt and pepper, and cook 5 minutes more, until the parsnips brown lightly. Remove from heat before stirring in the yogurt, chutney, and cilantro.

Serves 4

1½ pounds parsnips, peeled and cut into bite-size pieces
2 tablespoons butter or oil
1 red onion, thinly sliced
2 Bosc pears or Golden Delicious apples, cored, thinly sliced
1 teaspoon Madras curry powder, toasted in a dry pan until fragrant
½ teaspoon ground coriander, toasted in a dry pan until fragrant
Kosher salt and black pepper
¼ cup yogurt
¼ cup mango chutney (such as Major Grey's)
2 tablespoons chopped cilantro

Black Bean–Cilantro Fritters

To add an extracrunchy exterior to these spicy, pressure cooker fritters, try rolling them in panko bread crumbs before frying.

Serves 8–10

1 cup black beans
8 cups water
1 tablespoon vegetable oil
1 teaspoon salt
1 red bell pepper, diced
1 jalapeño, minced
½ cup onion, diced
¼ cup chopped cilantro
1 cup flour
1 cup cornmeal
1 tablespoon baking powder
½ cup heavy cream or unsweetened soymilk
2 eggs, beaten, or 2 teaspoons cornstarch mixed with 2 tablespoons water
2 quarts canola oil, for frying
Salt and pepper, to taste

1. Add the beans and 4 cups water to the pressure cooker. Lock the lid into place; bring to high pressure for 1 minute. Remove from heat and quick-release the pressure.

2. Drain the water, rinse the beans, and add to the pressure cooker again with the remaining 4 cups water. Soak for 1 hour.

3. Add the vegetable oil and salt. Lock the lid into place; bring to high pressure and maintain for 12 minutes. Remove from heat and allow pressure to release naturally. Drain and set aside.

4. In a bowl, combine the red bell pepper, jalapeño, onion, cilantro, and black beans.

5. In another bowl combine the flour, cornmeal, baking powder, heavy cream or soymilk, and 2 eggs or cornstarch mixture. Add the vegetable and bean mixture to the flour mixture and stir until well combined. Form the batter into 1" fritters.

6. In a large pot, heat the oil to 350°F and fry the fritters until golden brown, about 3–4 minutes.

Chana Masala

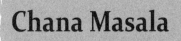

The main ingredient in this popular slow cooker Indian dish is chickpeas.

Add all ingredients to a 4-quart slow cooker. Cover and cook on low heat for 6 hours.

Serves 8

2 (15-ounce) cans chickpeas, drained
1 cup water
4 teaspoons salt
¼ cup butter or vegan margarine
1 onion, diced
5 cloves garlic, minced
1 tablespoon cumin
½ teaspoon cayenne pepper
1 teaspoon ground turmeric
2 teaspoons paprika
1 teaspoon garam masala
1 cup tomatoes, diced
1 lemon, juiced
2 teaspoons grated fresh ginger

Spicy Black-Eyed Peas and Kale

The black-eyed peas in this spicy, slow cooker recipe are good sources of fiber, protein, and iron.

Serves 8

1 (16-ounce) bag dried black-eyed peas

Enough water to cover black-eyed peas by 1"

4 teaspoons salt

2 tablespoons olive oil

1 onion, diced

5 cloves garlic, minced

1 pound kale, chopped

½ teaspoon cayenne pepper

2 teaspoons cumin

1 teaspoon black pepper

1. Rinse the black-eyed peas, then soak overnight. Drain the water and rinse the peas again.

2. In a large pot, add the peas and cover with water. Boil on high heat for 10 minutes, then drain.

3. Add black-eyed peas, water, and 2 teaspoons salt to a 4-quart slow cooker. Cover and cook on medium heat for about 5–6 hours. Check the black-eyed peas at about 5 hours and continue cooking if necessary.

4. Once the black-eyed peas are done, drain in a colander.

5. Add the olive oil to the slow cooker and sauté the onion, garlic, and kale for about 5 minutes.

6. Add the rest of the ingredients, including the black-eyed peas, to the slow cooker. Cover and allow to cook for 15–20 minutes more.

Red Bean Fritters

Serve these hot and spicy, pressure cooker fritters with a side of sour cream or vegan sour cream, for dipping.

1. Add the beans and 4 cups water to the pressure cooker. Lock the lid into place; bring to high pressure for 1 minute. Remove from heat and quick-release the pressure.

2. Drain the water, rinse the beans, and add to the pressure cooker again with the remaining 4 cups water. Soak for 1 hour.

3. Add the olive oil and salt. Lock the lid into place; bring to high pressure and maintain for 11 minutes. Remove from heat and allow pressure to release naturally. Drain and set aside.

4. In a bowl, combine the jalapeño, onion, garlic, cilantro, and red beans.

5. In another bowl combine the flour, cornmeal, baking powder, heavy cream or soymilk, and 2 eggs or cornstarch mixture. Add the bean mixture to the flour mixture and stir until well combined. Form the batter into 1" fritters.

6. In a large pot, heat the canola oil to 350°F and fry the fritters until golden brown, about 3–4 minutes.

Serves 6–8

1 cup red beans
8 cups water
1 tablespoon olive oil
1 teaspoon salt
1 jalapeño, minced
½ onion, diced
4 cloves garlic, minced
¼ cup chopped cilantro
1 cup flour
1 cup cornmeal
1 tablespoon baking powder
½ cup heavy cream or unsweetened soymilk
2 eggs, beaten, or 2 teaspoons cornstarch mixed with 2 tablespoons water
2 quarts canola oil, for frying
Salt and pepper, to taste

Chickpeas in Potato-Onion Curry

Thirty-minute main dishes like this are a lifesaver when you come home hungry and nothing's ready. Put on a pot of basmati rice before you start this dish, and you'll be dining on this spicy deliciousness before you know it.

Serves 4

2 cups onions, cut into 1" pieces
3 tablespoons oil, divided
1½ cups cubed (1") potatoes
1 (14-ounce) can coconut milk
1 (15-ounce) can chickpeas (garbanzos), drained and rinsed
5–6 cloves garlic, peeled
1 teaspoon kosher salt
1½ teaspoons ground coriander
½ teaspoon ground turmeric
1 teaspoon chili powder
1 teaspoon ground cumin
Juice of ½ a lemon

1. In a skillet over high heat, cook the onions in 1 tablespoon oil until lightly browned, about 5 minutes. Add the potatoes and coconut milk; cover and cook until potatoes are tender, about 20 minutes; add the chickpeas. In a food processor, combine the garlic, salt, coriander, turmeric, chili powder, and cumin; process until it becomes a paste, scraping down sides as needed.

2. Heat remaining oil in a small skillet and fry the garlic mixture for 1 minute, allowing it to become fragrant and slightly browned. Add the garlic mixture to the chickpea pot. Simmer for 2 to 3 minutes; season to taste with lemon and additional salt. Serve with basmati rice and/or Indian breads.

Curried Green Beans

Green beans taste great just barely cooked and with plenty of snap. But in this instance, you have to cook the beans until they are soft. As the beans break down, they help form the sauce.

1. In a large saucepan, heat the vegetable oil over medium-high heat.

2. Add the curry paste and stir-fry for 1 minute.

3. Stir in the Vegetable Stock until well combined with the paste. Add the green beans and bring to a low boil. Cook for 15–20 minutes to reduce the liquid.

4. Reduce the heat to maintain a hard simmer and continue cooking until the beans are very well done.

5. Serve the beans over steamed rice, ladling the sauce over the top.

Serves 4–6

2 tablespoons vegetable oil
3 tablespoons Red Curry Paste (see Chapter 2)
6 cups Vegetable Stock (see Chapter 5)
1 pound green beans, trimmed

CHAPTER 7

Vegetables

Savory Turnip Greens

In this spicy, pressure cooker recipe be sure to use fresh or frozen turnip greens for best flavor and optimal nutrition.

Serves 4

1 pound turnip greens
1 tablespoon olive oil
½ onion, diced
1 garlic clove, minced
1 teaspoon dried red pepper flakes
2 cups Vegetable Stock (see Chapter 5)
1 teaspoon Dijon mustard
Salt and pepper, to taste

1. To prepare the greens, cut away the tough stalks and stems. Wash greens, chop into large pieces, and set aside.

2. Bring the pressure cooker to medium heat. Add the olive oil, onion, garlic, and red pepper flakes. Cook until the onion begins to soften, about 5 minutes. Add the Vegetable Stock, mustard, and chopped greens; stir well.

3. Lock the lid into place and bring to high pressure; maintain for 5 minutes. Remove from heat and release pressure naturally. Add salt and pepper, to taste.

Moroccan Root Vegetables

This spicy, slow cooker recipe is good served with couscous and a yogurt or a side salad.

1. Add the parsnips, turnips, onions, carrots, apricots, prunes, turmeric, cumin, ginger, cinnamon, cayenne pepper, parsley, and cilantro to a 4-quart slow cooker.

2. Pour in the Vegetable Stock and salt.

3. Cover and cook on low for 9 hours, or until the vegetables are cooked through.

Serves 8

1 pound parsnips, peeled and diced
1 pound turnips, peeled and diced
2 medium onions, chopped
1 pound carrots, peeled and diced
6 dried apricots, chopped
4 pitted prunes, chopped
1 teaspoon ground turmeric
1 teaspoon ground cumin
½ teaspoon ground ginger
½ teaspoon ground cinnamon
¼ teaspoon ground cayenne pepper
1 tablespoon dried parsley
1 tablespoon dried cilantro
2 cups Vegetable Stock (see Chapter 5)
1 teaspoon salt

Potato Messaround

"Messaround" means a little bit of everything, which is what this slow cooker recipe has! Try playing with it by adding different cheeses and hot peppers or swap out the Vegetable Stock and soup, to your taste.

Serves 4

8 cups red potatoes, cubed
1 red onion, diced
1 poblano pepper, diced
1 red pepper, diced
1 jalapeño pepper, minced
3 cups Vegetable Stock (see
   Chapter 5)
1 (14½-ounce) can cream of
   mushroom soup or vegan
   cream of mushroom soup
1 teaspoon salt
¼ teaspoon black pepper
1 cup shredded Cheddar cheese
   or vegan Cheddar
2 tablespoons chives

1. Add all of the ingredients to a 4-quart slow cooker except for the chives.

2. Cover and cook on high heat for 4–5 hours. Garnish with the chives.

Slow Cooker Potatoes Paprikash

This Hungarian classic is the perfect spicy side dish to serve with a seitan roast.

1. In a nonstick pan, heat the oil. Add the onion, shallot, and garlic and sauté for 1–2 minutes, or until they begin to soften. Add the salt, caraway seeds, pepper, cayenne, and paprika, and stir. Immediately remove from heat.

2. Add the onion mixture, potatoes, Vegetable Stock, and tomato paste to a 4-quart slow cooker. Stir to coat the potatoes evenly.

3. Cover and cook on high for 2½ hours, or until the potatoes are tender.

4. Turn off the heat and stir in the sour cream.

Serves 8

1½ teaspoons olive oil
1 medium onion, halved and sliced
1 shallot, minced
4 cloves garlic, minced
½ teaspoon salt
½ teaspoon caraway seeds
¼ teaspoon freshly ground black pepper
1 teaspoon cayenne
3 tablespoons paprika
2 pounds red potatoes, thinly sliced
2 cups Vegetable Stock (see Chapter 5)
2 tablespoons tomato paste
½ cup reduced-fat sour cream or vegan sour cream

Southwestern Casserole

Unless you're vegan, serve this delicious, spicy, slow cooker dish with a poached egg on top.

Serves 6

4 large red potatoes, diced
1 (15-ounce) can black beans, drained
1 large onion, diced
1 jalapeño, seeded and diced
1 tablespoon butter or vegan margarine
1 (15-ounce) can diced tomatoes
4 ounces button mushrooms, sliced
¼ teaspoon salt
¼ teaspoon pepper
¼ cup shredded Mexican-blend cheese or vegan Cheddar

1. In a 4-quart slow cooker, stir all ingredients together except the cheese.

2. Cover and cook on low for 8–9 hours.

3. Stir in the cheese shortly before serving.

Mexican Spice Potatoes

If you like things spicy, really kick this slow cooker recipe up a notch by adding an extra teaspoon of cayenne to these potatoes!

Add all ingredients to a 4-quart slow cooker. Cover and cook on high heat for 4 hours.

Serves 4

6 cups red potatoes, cubed
1 teaspoon chili powder
½ teaspoon sugar
½ teaspoon paprika
⅛ teaspoon cayenne pepper
⅛ teaspoon garlic powder
¼ teaspoon cumin
½ teaspoon salt
⅛ teaspoon black pepper
½ cup water

Spicy Chipotle and Thyme Mashed Sweet Potatoes

To substitute fresh thyme for dried thyme in this spicy pressure cooker recipe, use ½ tablespoon of the fresh herb.

Serves 4–6

2 cups water
6 cups sweet potatoes, cubed
4 tablespoons butter or vegan margarine, such as Earth Balance
3 cloves garlic, minced
½ teaspoon dried chipotle pepper
½ teaspoon dried thyme
Salt and pepper, to taste

1. Pour water into the pressure cooker and add potatoes. Lock the lid into place and bring to high pressure. Once achieved, turn the heat to low and cook for 5 minutes. Remove from heat and release pressure naturally.

2. Drain the potatoes into a colander. Add the butter or margarine to the pressure cooker and sauté the garlic for about 2 minutes. Remove the pressure cooker from the heat. Add the sweet potatoes, chipotle pepper, and thyme. Mash the potatoes using a potato masher or electric mixer. Season with salt and pepper, to taste.

Aloo Gobi (Cauliflower and Potato Curry)

This hot and spicy North Indian curry is a hearty main course. It's also an excellent filling for wraps known as roti.

1. Cut the cauliflower and potatoes into large chunks. Heat the oil in a heavy skillet over medium-high heat, and cook the onions, chilies, and ginger until brown, about 10 minutes. Add the tomatoes, chili powder, turmeric, coriander, and salt; cook 5 minutes more, until spices are fragrant and evenly disbursed. Mix in the potatoes and cauliflower, plus enough water to come halfway up the vegetables.

2. Cover the pan and cook for 20 minutes, stirring occasionally, until the potatoes and cauliflower are very tender. Add the garam masala powder; cook 5 minutes more. Serve garnished with cilantro or parsley.

Serves 8

1 large head cauliflower
2 pounds potatoes
3 tablespoons oil
2 large onions, finely chopped (about 5 cups)
4 jalapeños or other chili peppers, finely chopped
1 (1") piece fresh ginger, finely chopped
3 tomatoes, finely chopped
1¼ teaspoons chili powder
1 teaspoon turmeric
1 teaspoon coriander
2 teaspoons kosher salt
1 teaspoon garam masala (spice mixture available at specialty stores—or make your own by combining 1 teaspoon each of ground cardamom, cumin seed, cloves, black pepper, and cinnamon)
Cilantro or parsley, chopped

Smoky Spiced Collard Greens with Turnip

The smokiness in this dish comes from the chipotle chili, a smoked jalapeño pepper, available dried or canned in most supermarkets in the Mexican foods section, or at Latino specialty markets. For milder greens, remove the seeds and veins from the chili before use.

Serves 4

1 bunch collards or turnip greens
1 medium white turnip, peeled and diced into ¼" pieces
1 medium onion, chopped
1 chipotle chili, dried or canned, cut in half
1 teaspoon salt
1 tablespoon olive oil
1 cup Vegetable Stock (see Chapter 5) or water

1. Wash greens and remove the stems. Cut leaves into long thin strips (julienne).

2. In a heavy-bottomed pot, sauté the turnip, onion, and chili in olive oil until the onion is translucent. Add the greens and salt, and sauté a few minutes more, until greens are wilted.

3. Add Vegetable Stock or water, bring to a boil, and reduce heat to simmer for 20 minutes, or until greens are very tender and turnips are soft.

Kimchi-Style Cabbage

If you can't find Korean chili powder to use in this pressure cooker dish, substitute plain chili powder, which is also made from crushed red peppers.

Add the garlic, ginger, scallions, water, soy sauce, and chili powder to the pressure cooker and stir well. Add the cabbage and carrots. Lock on the lid. Bring to high pressure; maintain pressure for 2 minutes. Remove the pan from the heat, quick-release the pressure, and remove the lid.

Yields 1 quart

1 clove garlic, minced
1 teaspoon fresh ginger, minced
1 bunch scallions, sliced
½ cup water
¼ cup soy sauce
1 tablespoon Korean chili powder
4 cups Napa cabbage, cut into 2" pieces
1 cup carrots, julienned

🔥 KIMCHI

Kimchi is a popular Korean condiment that is often used as the base for other recipes. Traditional recipes call for fermenting the mixture until pickled, but you can make "kimchi-style" cabbage by pressure-cooking the ingredients instead of fermenting.

Kale with Crushed Red Pepper

The antioxidant-rich dark leafy greens found in this spicy dish are nutritional powerhouses loaded with calcium, beta carotene, and vitamin C. They're also high in fiber and phytochemicals. One could say they're the liver of the vegetable world!

Serves 4

2 pounds kale, stems and ribs removed

1 tablespoon olive oil

1 medium red onion, chopped

1 tablespoon chopped garlic

2 tablespoons of crushed red pepper

2 teaspoons chopped fresh thyme leaves or ½ teaspoon dried

¼ cup dry sherry or white wine

Salt and freshly ground black pepper

Grated Parmesan cheese (optional; not vegan)

1. Bring a large pot of well-salted water to a rolling boil. Add the kale and cook for 10 minutes, until it has lost its waxy coating and the leaves are tender. Transfer to a colander to drain, reserving about ½ cup of the cooking liquid. Roughly chop the kale.

2. Heat the oil in a large skillet or Dutch oven. Add the onion, garlic, red pepper, and thyme. Cook over medium heat until the onion is soft and starting to brown around the edges. Splash in the sherry; cook for 5 minutes until all alcohol has evaporated. Add back the kale; cook 10 minutes more. Season with salt and pepper. Serve sprinkled with grated Parmesan cheese if desired.

Pressure Cooker Kale with Red Pepper Flakes and Cumin

The kale used in this spicy pressure cooker dish can be enjoyed while still tough and chewy, or completely softened. Adjust cooking times to reach the consistency you enjoy.

1. Bring water to a boil in the pressure cooker. Stir in ½ teaspoon salt. Blanch kale for 1 minute, drain, and set aside.

2. Add the olive oil to the pressure cooker over low heat. Add the garlic and red pepper flakes; cook for 30 seconds. Add the Vegetable Stock, cumin, and kale, then stir.

3. Lock the lid into place and bring to high pressure; maintain pressure for 6 minutes. Remove from heat and allow pressure to release naturally. Serve.

Serves 4

2 cups water
½ teaspoon salt, plus more to taste
8 cups kale, washed, drained, and chopped
1 tablespoon olive oil
1 clove garlic, minced
1 teaspoon dried red pepper flakes
½ cup Vegetable Stock (see Chapter 5)
½ teaspoon cumin

Szechuan Stir-Fried Cabbage with Hot Peppers

The spices in this Chinese cabbage dish are so delectable that they can make you forget about anything and everything else!

Serves 4–6

¼ cup, plus 2 tablespoons peanut or other neutral oil

8 dried red chili peppers, quartered and seeded

1 (1") piece fresh ginger, peeled and finely chopped

1 medium head cabbage (preferably Chinese cabbage, but any variety is okay), washed and chopped into 2" pieces

½ teaspoon cornstarch

1 tablespoon soy sauce

1 teaspoon dry sherry or Chinese cooking wine

1 teaspoon sugar

1 teaspoon rice wine vinegar

1 teaspoon Asian sesame oil

1. Heat ¼ cup of the oil in a wok or skillet over high heat. Stir in the peppers and fry, stirring, for 1 minute, until the peppers darken in color. Transfer the peppers and oil to a bowl and set aside.

2. Pour remaining 2 tablespoons of oil into the wok; add the ginger and cook for a few seconds until fragrant. Add the cabbage all at once. Fry, stirring, for 1 minute. Combine the cornstarch, soy sauce, and sherry or cooking wine in a small bowl. Add to the wok. Stir until the cornstarch cooks and forms a thick sauce; add the sugar and vinegar. Sprinkle in the sesame oil and pour in the red peppers and their oil. Stir to combine well. Transfer to a serving bowl.

Cabbage with Paprika

Apples give this earthy, spicy dish a bit of sweetness, while the cream gives it a cooling effect.

1. Melt the butter in a skillet. Add the onions and cook at a low-medium heat until they are softened, about 5 minutes.

2. Add the paprika, chili flakes, and cabbage, and stir. Cook over high heat for 2–3 minutes. Lower the heat, add the Vegetable Stock, cover, and let simmer for 20–25 minutes until cabbage is soft.

3. Add the apple to the pan, mix well, and cook until apple is heated through, another 3–4 minutes. Remove pan from heat.

4. Combine cream, paprika, and salt in a small bowl.

5. Transfer cabbage to serving dish and pour cream over cabbage. Serve.

Serves 4

3 tablespoons butter
2 onions, chopped
½ teaspoon hot paprika
Pinch red pepper flakes
1½ pounds cabbage, shredded or very thinly sliced
½ cup Vegetable Stock (see Chapter 5)
1 apple, peeled, cored, and thinly sliced
1 cup light cream
Pinch of paprika
Pinch of salt

Spiced "Baked" Eggplant

Serve this slow cooker Spiced "Baked" Eggplant as a main dish over rice or as a side dish as is.

Serves 4

1 pound eggplant, cubed
⅓ cup onion, sliced
2 teaspoons red pepper flakes
½ teaspoon crushed rosemary
¼ cup lemon juice

Place all ingredients in a 1½- to 2-quart slow cooker. Cook on low for 3 hours, or until the eggplant is tender.

🔥 COLD SNAP

Take care not to put a cold ceramic slow cooker insert directly into the slow cooker. The sudden shift in temperature can cause it to crack. If you want to prepare your ingredients the night before use, refrigerate them in reusable containers, not in the insert.

Cilantro-Lime Corn on the Cob

This pressure cooker Cilantro-Lime Corn on the Cob recipe couldn't be easier—or more delicious! To add a little more kick, increase the amount of cayenne pepper.

1. Place the rack in the pressure cooker and place the corn on the rack. Pour in the water.

2. Lock the lid into place and bring to low pressure; maintain pressure for 3 minutes. Remove the pressure cooker from heat, quick-release the pressure, and remove the lid.

3. In a small bowl, combine the butter or margarine, cilantro, lime juice, salt, and cayenne pepper until well blended.

4. When the corn is cool enough to handle, spread ¼ of the mixture on each ear of corn.

Serves 4

4 ears fresh sweet corn, shucked
½ cup water
2 tablespoons butter or vegan margarine, such as Earth Balance
2 tablespoons cilantro, chopped
2 teaspoons fresh lime juice
½ teaspoon salt
2 teaspoons cayenne pepper

Corn and Pepper Pudding

Serve this dish warm. It's a perfect side for any meal!

Serves 6

2 tablespoons unsalted butter, melted

3 cups cubed bread, about ½" dice

3 poblano peppers, roasted and peeled, and then diced

6 ears sweet corn, shucked, kernels cut off with a knife (about 3 cups)

¼ cup chopped chives

1 teaspoon salt

½ teaspoon freshly ground black pepper

4 eggs

2 cups milk

¾ cup shredded jalapeño pepper jack cheese

1. Heat oven to 350°F. Combine the melted butter and bread cubes; bake in a single layer until lightly browned, about 10 minutes. In a mixing bowl, combine the roasted peppers, corn, chives, bread cubes, salt, and pepper. Transfer to a buttered 8" × 11" baking dish.

2. Whisk together the eggs and milk; pour over bread mixture. Allow to sit for 10 minutes, to let the bread absorb the custard; top with the shredded cheese. Bake until set in the center and lightly browned on top, about 1 hour.

Stuffed Piquillo Peppers

Piquillo peppers are grown only in Navarre in northern Spain, where the freshly picked peppers are grilled over beech wood fires and packed in oil. They have a wonderful spicy, sweet, and smoky flavor.

1. Combine the goat cheese, pepper flakes, and garlic in a small bowl.

2. Using your fingers, carefully open each of the piquillo peppers at the stem end.

3. Gently stuff each with about ½ teaspoon of goat cheese mixture. Place peppers in a single layer on a baking dish. Pour the olive oil over the peppers.

4. Set the broiler to high. Broil the peppers for 8–10 minutes, or until the cheese is soft and bubbly.

5. Sprinkle with salt and pepper and serve.

Serves 4–6 as an appetizer

5 ounces goat cheese, brought to room temperature
½ teaspoon red pepper flakes
1 garlic clove, finely chopped
2 (12-ounce) jars of Spanish piquillo peppers, drained
3 tablespoons olive oil
Salt and pepper, to taste

Spicy Okra and Tomatoes

Generally, people either love okra or hate it—there's almost no in between. Native to Africa and used in southern United States cooking, okra pods add unique color and texture to the dinner table. Look for pods that are uniform in color, without any dark or soft spots.

Serves 4

1½ pounds okra, cut into 1" pieces

2 tablespoons vegetable oil

2 medium onions, thinly sliced

½ teaspoon fresh ginger, finely minced

2 tomatoes, seeded and roughly chopped

2 Thai (bird's eye) chilies, seeded and finely chopped

2 garlic cloves, peeled and finely minced

Salt and pepper, to taste

1. Bring a saucepan of salted water to a boil. Add the okra, lower the heat, and let simmer for about 3–4 minutes. Drain okra and set aside.

2. Over high heat, heat the oil in a large frying pan. Add the onions, ginger, tomatoes, and chilies, and sauté until the onions are soft and fragrant, about 5 minutes.

3. Lower the heat to medium, add the garlic, and sauté until garlic is soft, another 3–4 minutes.

4. Add the okra, salt and pepper, to taste, and cook until okra is just heated through, about 2–3 minutes.

🌶 WHAT MAKES OKRA SLIMY?

One of the reasons people are turned off by okra is because it has a natural slime. (There's no polite way to put it.) Okra is part of the mallow family, a group of plants that exude a gelatinous substance when cut. The slime is perfectly edible and, some might say, pleasant. Give it a try—you might even come to like it.

Zucchini with Chermoula

This dish packs a wonderful amount of flavor and, even better, takes very little effort to make. Instead of baking, feel free to pan-fry or grill the zucchini.

1. Wash the zucchinis, cut off the ends, then slice them lengthwise into ¼" thick pieces.

2. Rub the zucchini slices with the Chermoula and let marinate for 15–20 minutes.

3. Heat the oven to 350°F. Place the zucchini on a cookie sheet or baking dish. Bake 30–40 minutes, until zucchini is cooked but still a bit firm.

4. Serve zucchini hot or cold.

Serves 4

1½ pounds small zucchinis
½ cup Chermoula (see Chapter 2)

Elotes

This Mexican version of corn on the cob, a popular street food, is downright addictive: spicy, tangy, smoky, and sweet. Add as little or as much chili powder as you like. Boiled corn works fine, but grilling will give it extra flavor.

Serves 4

4 ears of corn, shucked and boiled or grilled
¼ cup unsalted butter, softened
¼ cup mayonnaise
1 teaspoon chili powder
½ cup grated Cotija or Parmesan cheese
1 lime, cut into wedges
Salt, to taste

1. Remove cooked corn from the water or the grill. Pat dry to get rid of any excess water.

2. Mix the softened butter with the mayonnaise and spread mixture over the corn cobs.

3. Sprinkle the corn with chili powder and grated cheese. Squirt lime over corn. Season to taste with salt.

🌶 COTIJA CHEESE

Cotija cheese is a hard cheese made from cow's milk that is found all over Mexico. It is dry and firm, crumbles easily, and has a delightfully salty flavor. If you can't find Cotija, you can substitute Parmesan for it. In fact, many street vendors in Mexico use the American standard Kraft Parmesan cheese from the green shaker.

Vinegar Pickled Peppers

You can use this basic brine for any kind of chili pepper. You could also use it for any vegetable; just add a few sliced chilies and a pinch of red pepper flakes for spicy pickles.

1. With a small paring knife, poke each pepper 2 or 3 times, creating small slits for the brine to seep in. Put peppers in a large, clean glass preserving jar or several smaller ones.

2. In a nonreactive saucepan, combine all remaining ingredients and bring to a boil. Reduce heat and let simmer for 2 minutes.

3. Remove brine from heat and pour over peppers. Screw the lid onto the jars and let cool.

4. When peppers are cool, put jars in the refrigerator and let sit for several days. You can eat them after just a few days, but they will taste better if you let them sit for at least a week.

Yields 20–25 peppers

1 pound fresh jalapeño peppers, washed
2½ cups water
2½ cups white vinegar
3 tablespoons kosher salt
1 tablespoon sugar
4 garlic cloves, peeled and thinly sliced
2 tablespoons coriander seeds
2 tablespoons black peppercorns
2 bay leaves

🔥 PICKLING SPICES

For extra flavor in your pickles, experiment with other spices you like from your pantry. Good options for pickling spices include: dried chilies, cinnamon sticks, mustard seeds, dill seeds, fennel seeds, allspice, cloves, and star anise. The best-tasting pickles are the ones that you create to suit your own preferences.

Salt Pickled Peppers

This simple recipe works best with fresh red chilies because the salt preserves their bright color and makes them especially striking. Feel free to use whatever kind of chilies you like, and consider adding other vegetables to the mix.

Yields 20–25 chilies

1 pound fresh red jalapeño peppers, washed
⅓ cup kosher salt

1. Make sure your chilies are thoroughly dried. Cut off the stems and tips and roughly chop them, keeping the seeds. It's a good idea to wear gloves for this task to avoid chili burns, as you'll be handling quite a few chilies.

2. Place the chopped chilies in a large bowl. Add the salt and mix thoroughly.

3. Place chilies in a large, clean glass jar or several smaller ones. Feel free to pack them to the top, as they will shrink in size. Fill in any excess space at the top with more salt.

4. Screw lids on tightly and leave in a cool place for 2 weeks before using. Once opened, store chilies in the refrigerator for several months.

♨ SALT PICKLES

When most people think of pickles, they think of vegetables floating in a vinegary brine. But pickles do not require vinegar and in much of the world, preserving is done simply with salt. Salt draws the moisture out of vegetables, which are made mostly of water, leaving behind crisp pickles with a clean, pure flavor.

Spicy Dill Pickles

A hotter take on the classic American dill pickle. Feel free to turn up the heat as you like.

1. Combine all ingredients except dill in a large bowl. Stir and let sit at room temperature for at least 2 hours.

2. Divide dill evenly into 2 or 3 jars. Divide cucumber spears evenly into jars as well.

3. Pour pickling liquid over cucumber spears.

4. Screw lids on and store in the refrigerator for 2 days before using.

Yields 48 pickles

12 pickling cucumbers (also called Kirbys), cut lengthwise into quarters
2 serrano peppers, thinly sliced
2 cups white vinegar
1½ cups water
1 tablespoon coriander seeds
1 tablespoon black peppercorns
1 teaspoon fennel seeds
1 teaspoon crushed red chili pepper flakes
1 bunch dill, roughly chopped

Rum Chilies

Try these on top of fish for a little spicy, Caribbean flair. Be sure to use gloves when handling the extremely spicy Scotch bonnet chilies.

Yields about 2 cups of pickles

1 tablespoon sugar
1 cup apple cider vinegar
2 bay leaves
1 teaspoon coriander seeds
1 teaspoon mustard seeds
1 red onion, thinly sliced
4 garlic cloves, peeled and thinly sliced
4 Scotch bonnet chilies, stem, seeds, and ribs removed, horizontally and thinly sliced (use habaneros if you can't find Scotch bonnets)
4 jalapeño peppers, seeds and ribs removed, thinly sliced
2 small carrots (or 1 large), thinly sliced
2 cups rum (preferably dark rum)

1. In a nonreactive saucepan, combine sugar, vinegar, bay leaves, coriander, and mustard. Bring to a boil, then reduce heat and let simmer for 5 minutes. Remove from heat and let cool.

2. Place onion, garlic, chilies, and carrots in a large, clean glass preserving jar or several smaller ones.

3. When the vinegar mixture has cooled, but is still warm, add the rum. Stir to combine, then pour mixture over chilies.

4. Screw lids on jars and store in the refrigerator for a few days before using.

🔥 PRESERVING IN ALCOHOL

Besides salt and vinegar, you can also preserve or "pickle" chilies in alcohol. Using alcohol is one of the simplest methods of preserving because it kills bacteria. Alcohols like rum have a high sugar content so they will give the chili peppers sweetness as well. Try pickling with vodka, gin, tequila, or even whiskey.

Spicy Chowchow

This sweet and spicy relish is a southern favorite. Try it alongside a meal with mashed potatoes.

1. In a large bowl, combine cabbage, jalapeños, peppers, tomatoes, and onions. Add the salt and stir well to combine. Cover and refrigerate for 6–8 hours, then rinse and drain well in a colander.

2. Put the vegetables into a large Dutch oven. Add the vinegar, sugar, celery, fennel, mustard, and turmeric. Bring to a boil, then reduce heat and simmer until vegetables are tender but not falling apart, about 1 hour.

3. Remove vegetables and let cool. Place in jars and store in the refrigerator for 2 weeks.

Yields 8 cups

½ head green cabbage, thinly shredded

10 jalapeño peppers, finely chopped (take out seeds and ribs for less heat)

3 red bell peppers, seeded and chopped

3 green bell peppers, seeded and chopped

3 green tomatoes, chopped

2 sweet onions, chopped

⅓ cup kosher salt

2 cups vinegar

1 cup sugar

2 teaspoons celery seed

2 teaspoons fennel seed

2 teaspoons mustard seed

2 teaspoons turmeric

🔥 CHOWCHOW

Chowchow is mainly known as a southern food, though a sweeter version of it is also found in Pennsylvania. It wasn't always southern, though. Chowchow migrated with the Acadian people after they were banished from Nova Scotia and settled in Louisiana.

Indian Mixed Pickles

These tangy, spicy pickles are traditionally served alongside most Indian meals. Try them on their own or with flatbread.

Yields about 2 cups of pickles

1 cup cauliflower, cut into small florets

2 shallots, cut horizontally into thin slices

1 large carrot, cut into thin strips

4 green jalapeño peppers, seeds and ribs removed, sliced lengthwise

1 thumb-size piece of fresh ginger, peeled and sliced into thin matchsticks

1 teaspoon salt

½ teaspoon cayenne pepper

½ teaspoon ground turmeric

3 teaspoons fresh lime juice

2 teaspoons mustard seeds

1 teaspoon fenugreek seeds

¼ cup vegetable oil

1. Mix all the vegetables together in a large, nonreactive bowl with salt, cayenne, turmeric, and lime juice. Set aside.

2. In a spice grinder, blend mustard and fenugreek seeds into a fine powder. Add to vegetables and stir to combine.

3. Pack vegetables into a clean glass preserving jar. Add oil.

4. Screw lid on jar and place in the refrigerator. Let sit for 2–3 days before using.

🔥 FENUGREEK

Fenugreek is a plant that can be used both as a spice (the seed) and an herb (the leaves). Fenugreek is used throughout Indian and South Asian cuisine, as well as in Ethiopian and Eritrean cooking. It adds an earthy flavor to curries and sauces and can be found in most Indian and Middle Eastern markets.

CHAPTER 8

Pasta Dishes

Fusilli (Spirals) with Grilled Eggplant, Garlic, and Spicy Tomato Sauce

Smoky, fruity flavors of grilled or roasted eggplant marry beautifully with tomatoes and garlic. Fusilli's deep crannies scoop up every drop of this spicy, complex sauce.

Serves 4

1 small eggplant (about ½ pound), cut lengthwise into 8 wedges
3 tablespoons olive oil, divided
Kosher salt and freshly ground black pepper
3 cloves garlic, finely chopped (about 1 tablespoon)
1 teaspoon crushed red pepper flakes
½ cup roughly chopped Italian parsley
4 cups tomato sauce
½ box (½ pound) fusilli or other pasta shape, cooked "al dente"
1 tablespoon butter (optional; not vegan)
¼ cup grated Parmesan cheese (optional; not vegan)

1. Heat grill, grill pan, or broiler. Toss the eggplant wedges with 1 tablespoon olive oil; season liberally with salt and pepper. Grill or broil wedges on the largest cut side for 4 minutes, until black marks show. Using tongs or a fork, turn to another side and cook 3 minutes more until they are bubbling with juices. Transfer to a cutting board to cool; cut into 1" pieces.

2. Mix remaining olive oil with garlic and red pepper flakes. Heat a large skillet over medium-high heat. Add the garlic mixture; allow to sizzle just 15 seconds, stirring with a wooden spoon, before adding the parsley. Cook 30 seconds; add the eggplant and tomato sauce. Bring to a simmer, add the cooked pasta, and cook until heated through; remove from heat. Finish by adding butter and cheese if using, adjusting for seasoning and tossing well to combine. Serve in bowls, sprinkled with additional chopped parsley. Serve additional cheese on the side if desired.

Orzo-Stuffed Poblano Peppers

Kick up the heat on these pressure cooker stuffed peppers even more by stirring cayenne pepper or minced pickled jalapeños into the orzo mixture.

1. Preheat the oven to 350°F. Fill the pressure cooker with enough water to cover the pasta. Bring the water to a boil. Add the pasta. Lock the lid into place and bring to high pressure; maintain pressure for 3 minutes. Use the natural-release method to release the pressure, then remove the lid.

2. In a medium bowl, combine the orzo, onions, tomatoes, garlic, cilantro, olive oil, salt, and pepper. Stir until combined.

3. Place the poblano peppers on a flat surface and cut out a long triangular portion from the top (stem to tip) to make room for the filling. Remove the seeds.

4. Fill each pepper with the orzo mixture and put the triangular piece of pepper back in place, covering the hole. Place on a baking sheet.

5. Bake for 45–50 minutes, or until tender.

Serves 4

Water, as needed
½ cup orzo pasta
¼ cup onions, diced
¼ cup tomatoes, diced
1 clove garlic, minced
2 tablespoons cilantro, chopped
1 tablespoon extra-virgin olive oil
Salt and pepper, to taste
4 large poblano peppers

🔥 ORZO PASTA

Orzo is a small rice-shaped pasta that is often used similarly to rice in cooking. It's a great alternative for chilled pasta salads, stuffing peppers or tomatoes, or tossed in a light sauce. Serving it with a heavy marinara or cream-based sauce is not recommended.

Pasta Puttanesca

Here's a sauce that's not shy on flavor: spicy, thanks to red chili, and salty, thanks to olives. Don't be surprised if you end up licking the bowl.

Serves 4

¼ cup olive oil
5 garlic cloves, peeled and roughly chopped
1 teaspoon crushed red pepper flakes
1 (35-ounce) can of tomatoes with their juices
½ cup chopped kalamata olives
1 pound of your favorite pasta (linguine and spaghetti are good choices here), cooked and drained
Handful fresh parsley, roughly chopped

1. Heat the olive oil in a wide saucepan. Add the garlic and red pepper flakes, and cook until garlic is softened about 4–5 minutes.

2. Add the tomatoes, stir, and break up the tomatoes with the spoon. Let simmer for 2–3 minutes.

3. Add the olives and stir. Let the sauce simmer and the flavors come together, about 5–10 minutes.

4. Put the cooked pasta in a bowl, add the sauce, and toss. Sprinkle with parsley.

🔥 THE LEGEND OF PUTTANESCA

The culinary legend behind puttanesca ("whore's-style sauce") is that it was devised by Italian prostitutes. The idea is that the deeply aromatic sauce would lure customers off the streets and into bordellos. This may or may not be true, but leave it to the people behind the oldest profession in the world to develop a dish that is popular to this day.

Spaghetti with Sweet Corn, Tomatoes, and Goat Cheese

Late summer is the perfect time to scoop up sweet seasonal vegetables like scallions, corn, and tomatoes and spicy peppers like jalapeños. When vegetables are ripe, they do all the work for you in a dish like this.

1. Cook the pasta according to the package directions. Heat the butter or oil in a large skillet over medium heat. Add the scallions, corn, red bell pepper, and jalapeño. Cook 3 minutes; add the tomatoes, cilantro, and ¼ cup water or Vegetable Stock. Season to taste.

2. Add the pasta. Sprinkle in the crumbled cheese and toss to distribute. Divide into 4 portions, and garnish with additional chopped cilantro and lemon wedges.

Serves 4

½ box (8 ounces) spaghetti
2 tablespoons butter or oil
4 scallions, chopped
2 cups fresh corn kernels (about 3 ears)
1 cup diced red bell pepper
1 jalapeño pepper, finely chopped
3 tomatoes, diced
¼ cup chopped cilantro
¼ cup water or Vegetable Stock (see Chapter 5)
Salt and pepper, to taste
2 ounces goat cheese, crumbled
1 lemon

Spicy Mac and Cheese

Any Mexican-style hot sauce such as Tapatío, Valentina, or Cholula would be a good choice for this recipe.

Serves 4

8 ounces small elbow macaroni
1¼ cups half-and-half
½ yellow onion, finely diced
3 teaspoons hot sauce of your choosing
2 cups grated Cheddar cheese
1½ tablespoons all-purpose flour
½ cup plain bread crumbs
½ teaspoon cayenne pepper

1. Cook macaroni in boiling salted water until just short of done. (Noodles should be al dente—slightly chewy.)

2. Heat oven to 400°F. Butter a 9" × 13" baking dish.

3. Bring half-and-half, onion, and hot sauce to a simmer in a large saucepan over medium heat.

4. Toss Cheddar cheese and flour together in a bowl so cheese is mostly coated; add mixture to half-and-half mixture. Whisk until sauce is smooth. Return sauce to simmer and let cook another 2–3 minutes.

5. Add pasta to sauce and stir to combine.

6. Spread pasta mixture into baking dish.

7. Toss bread crumbs with cayenne pepper in a small bowl. Sprinkle on top of pasta.

8. Bake mac and cheese until heated through and bread crumbs begin to brown, about 20–30 minutes.

Spaghetti with Garlic and Chili Oil

This is a simple recipe, but one that you will come back to again and again. The garlic and chilies infuse the oil with a rich flavor.

1. Heat the oil in a small pan, then add the garlic, chili, and pepper flakes, and cook over low heat for 2–3 minutes, until the garlic turns golden brown. Remove the pan from the heat and set aside.

2. Cook the spaghetti in a large pot of salted water.

3. Drain the pasta and put in a large bowl. Add the garlic and chili oil and parsley, and toss.

4. Top with grated cheese and serve.

Serves 4

6 tablespoons olive oil
3 garlic cloves, peeled and thinly
    sliced lengthwise
1 fresh serrano chili (seeded, if
    you like), thinly sliced
Pinch of crushed red pepper
    flakes
1 pound spaghetti
Salt, to taste
½ bunch of fresh parsley leaves,
    finely chopped
Grated Parmesan cheese, for
    garnish

Linguine with Jalapeño Pesto

This pesto can be tossed with some hot cooked pasta for an instant lunch, or mixed with sour cream for an easy appetizer. It also freezes well in ice cube trays, and keeps for about three months when frozen.

Yields 2 cups

½ cup pumpkin seeds
1 tablespoon vegetable oil
½ cup chopped onion
2 cloves garlic, minced
5 jalapeño peppers
1 cup cilantro leaves
1 cup flat leaf parsley
2 tablespoons lime juice
½ teaspoon salt
¼ teaspoon pepper
½ cup olive oil
⅓ cup grated Manchego or
 Romano cheese
1 pound linguine

1. In small skillet, toast pumpkin seeds over medium heat until light brown and fragrant. Remove to kitchen towel to cool. In same skillet, heat vegetable oil and sauté onion and garlic until tender. Remove to blender or food processor bowl.

2. Add cooled seeds, jalapeños, cilantro, parsley, lime juice, salt, and pepper and blend or process until finely chopped. With motor running, add olive oil in a thin stream until a paste forms. Remove to bowl and stir in cheese.

3. Cook the linguine in a large pot of salted water. Drain the pasta and put in a large bowl. Top with Jalapeño Pesto.

🔥 NUT SUBSTITUTIONS

Other nuts can be substituted for pumpkin seeds. Peanuts, pine nuts, and slivered almonds have about the same texture and similar flavor. For a richer flavor, use pecans or cashews. Remember to let all nuts cool thoroughly after roasting and before chopping or processing, or they will be soggy.

Koshary

Koshary is one of Egypt's national dishes. Koshary is a perfect match for Harissa (see Chapter 2).

1. Begin caramelizing your onions. They will take a bit of time, so start them first and keep an eye on them.

2. Put the lentils in a pot and cover with water, seasoning with salt and pepper. Bring lentils to a boil, then turn heat to medium and let boil until tender, about 30 minutes. Drain.

3. Combine rice with 1½ cups water in a pot. Cover, bring to a boil, turn heat to low, then let simmer till done, about 15 minutes.

4. Cook macaroni in boiling water until done. Drain.

5. Heat olive oil in the bottom of a saucepan, add garlic and spices, and sauté until garlic is soft and fragrant. Add tomato sauce and vinegar, and let simmer on stove for 10 minutes or so.

6. Check on caramelized onions. When they are done, remove from heat and set aside.

7. Assemble Koshary, starting with a scoop of rice, then a scoop of lentils. Add a layer of macaroni, then cover with tomato sauce. Top with caramelized onions. Serve with a dollop of Harissa hot sauce.

Serves 4

2 large onions, thinly sliced
1 cup brown lentils, picked through for stones
Salt and pepper, to taste
1 cup long-grain white rice
1½ cups water
1 cup elbow macaroni
2 tablespoons olive oil
2 garlic cloves, peeled and finely chopped
½ teaspoon cumin
½ teaspoon coriander
½ teaspoon crushed red pepper flakes
2½ cups tomato sauce (homemade or from a can)
2 tablespoons white or red wine vinegar

Sriracha Noodles

Sriracha adds a wonderful kick to this noodle dish. If you'd like to jazz things up by adding in your favorite protein feel free to make the change.

Serves 4

Sauce

2 tablespoons white vinegar
¼ cup curry powder
¼ cup soy sauce
1 cup vegetarian oyster sauce
¼ cup sriracha sauce
¼ cup ketchup

Remaining Ingredients

2 gallons water
1 pound rice stick noodles
4 tablespoons canola oil
1 tablespoon chopped garlic
1 cup julienned cabbage
½ cup julienned carrots
2 medium diced tomatoes
1 bunch sliced green onions
⅓ cup shallots
¼ bunch roughly chopped
   cilantro
Juice of 1 lime
1 teaspoon sesame oil

1. In a bowl, combine all the ingredients for the sauce, mix well, and set aside.

2. Bring water to a rolling boil. Place rice sticks in boiling water for 2 minutes. Drain, then rinse under rapid running hot water for 1 minute, and drain well again. Toss noodles with 2 tablespoons of canola oil and set aside.

3. In a hot wok, stir-fry garlic, cabbage, carrots, and tomatoes for 1 minute.

4. Add noodles and stir-fry 1 minute more.

5. Add sauce and stir-fry until ingredients are well incorporated, about 2 minutes. Add onions, shallots, cilantro, lime juice, and sesame oil and toss briefly.

CHAPTER 9

Hot and Spicy Desserts and Drinks

DESSERTS

Spicy Fruit Salad

Mango Chili Sorbet

Red Chili Ice Cream

Mexican Hot Chocolate

Bourbon and Chili Brownies

Louisiana Praline Pecans

Spicy Banana Pops

Spiced Chocolate Cake

Spiced Peaches

DRINKS

Bloody Mary Mix

Bloody Maria

Micheladas

Cucumber Margaritas

Hot-Blooded

Prairie Fire Shooter

Spicy Fruit Salad

Tropical fruit sprinkled with chili powder is a popular street snack in Mexico. Consider this a basic guide, and use any amount and combination of fruits that you like. It's impossible to screw this up.

Yields as many servings as you like

Pineapple, peeled, cored, and cut into cubes

Mangoes, peeled, cored, and cut into cubes

Watermelon, skin removed, cut into cubes

Papaya, peeled, cored, and cut into cubes

Jicama, peeled and cut into cubes

Fresh lime juice, to taste

Chili powder, to taste

Salt, to taste

1. Place all the fruit in a large, shallow bowl.

2. Squeeze lime juice all over the fruit. Sprinkle generously with chili powder, then sprinkle with salt.

3. Stir the fruit gently to mix ingredients without bruising fruit.

4. Taste and adjust seasoning to your liking.

♨ JICAMA

Jicama (pronounced "HEE-ka-ma") is a common Mexican ingredient. It's a root vegetable that has a thin brown skin and a crunchy white flesh. It has a mild flavor that is both sweet and earthy. It can be eaten raw or cooked, but when used raw it adds a refreshing crunch and snap to dishes like salad.

Mango Chili Sorbet

Based on the Mexican fruit with chili snack, this nondairy ice frozen treat is perfect on a hot day. For ultrasmooth ice, purée the mixture two or three times. Or just enjoy it chunky.

1. Put all ingredients in a blender and process until smooth. You may need to add just a little bit of water.

2. Pour mixture into large bowl. Cover and put in freezer for 2 hours.

3. Take the mixture out of the freezer and purée in blender again.

4. Freeze mixture again until solid. Serve with an extra sprinkling of chili powder.

Yields 4 servings

8 large mangoes, peeled, pitted, and cut into small cubes
2 cups sugar
¾ cup fresh lime juice
½ teaspoon ancho chili powder

🔥 MANGOES

Mangoes are a tropical fruit than have been cultivated since as far back as 2000 B.C. in India. Today, they are cultivated throughout Southeast Asia, Mexico, South America, and the Caribbean. Because they continue to ripen even after they are picked, mangoes are a popular export crop and have no trouble making long journeys to their final destinations.

Red Chili Ice Cream

The ice cream may be cold, but the cayenne pepper and cinnamon in it will give your tongue an unmistakably warm feeling. The heat level here is mild to medium, but feel free to punch it up by adding even more cayenne pepper.

Yields 1 quart

1 cup whole milk
2 cups heavy cream
¾ cup granulated sugar
1 cinnamon stick
6 egg yolks
½ teaspoon ground cayenne pepper

1. In a medium, heavy-bottomed saucepan, combine milk, heavy cream, sugar, and cinnamon stick. Heat until scalding, then remove from heat, cover, and let mixture infuse for 1 hour.

2. In a bowl, stir together the egg yolks.

3. Remove the cinnamon stick from the milk and rewarm the milk at a low temperature. Gradually pour some of the milk into the egg yolks, whisking constantly. Return the warmed yolks and milk back to the saucepan.

4. Add the cayenne pepper and cook mixture over low heat, stirring constantly. Scrape the bottom of the pan as you stir, heating until the custard is thick enough to coat the back of a spoon.

5. Remove mixture from heat and let cool completely. Place the mixture in the refrigerator to chill thoroughly, overnight if possible.

6. After mixture is cooled, freeze it in your ice cream maker according to the manufacturer's instructions.

Mexican Hot Chocolate

Few things are more comforting on a winter night than a cup of hot cocoa, except this hot cocoa with a little extra spice.

1. Over medium heat, combine all the ingredients in a large saucepan. Whisk constantly until mixture is hot, but not boiling, about 6–8 minutes.

2. Pour into mugs.

Serves 4

4 cups whole milk
½ cup water
8 ounces bittersweet chocolate, finely chopped (you could also use chocolate chips)
2 tablespoons sugar
1 teaspoon vanilla extract
½ teaspoon chili powder
¼ teaspoon ground cinnamon
Pinch of kosher salt

🌶 THE SKINNY ON WHOLE MILK

Whole milk, 2%, 1%, and skim—what's the difference? These numbers and names refer to the amount of fat that is found in the milk. While calling it whole makes it seem like it's made entirely of fat, the truth is it is about 3.5 percent milk fat. Obviously, 2% and 1% contain those amounts of fat, respectively. The difference is not that big on the calorie front either, with one 8-ounce serving of whole milk containing about 146 calories, while 2% holds 122, 1% holds 102, and skim contains 86.

Bourbon and Chili Brownies

This recipe yields dense, chewy brownies with spicy hints of chili and bourbon.

Yields 1 dozen big brownies

4 ounces bittersweet chocolate, roughly chopped
1 stick unsalted butter, softened, and cut into little cubes
1 cup sugar
2 eggs
½ teaspoon vanilla extract
¼ cup bourbon
½ cup, plus 1 tablespoon all-purpose flour
⅛ teaspoon salt
¼ teaspoon cinnamon
½ teaspoon ancho chili powder

1. Preheat oven to 350°F. Grease an 8" square baking pan.

2. Combine chocolate and butter in a small, microwavable bowl. Microwave 20 seconds at a time until melted, and stir until smooth. (You can also melt the chocolate and butter in a small saucepan on the stove.)

3. Transfer chocolate mixture to a large bowl. Add sugar and stir to combine.

4. Add eggs, one at a time, stirring after each until smooth.

5. Add vanilla extract and bourbon, then stir.

6. Add flour, salt, cinnamon, and chili powder. Stir gently until smooth.

7. Pour mixture into baking pan and bake 20–25 minutes, until it is just set in the middle and a toothpick stuck in comes out clean.

8. Let cool before cutting into 12 brownies.

Louisiana Praline Pecans

These sweet tidbits are made from whole individual (shelled) pecans with a rum praline coating on each one.

1. Preheat oven to 350°F.

2. Combine the cream, rum, and Tabasco in a bowl. Add the pecans and stir to coat. Add the brown sugar and toss with a fork to coat the pecans.

3. Pour the coated pecans onto a baking sheet lined with nonstick foil and separate them into individual nuts with a fork.

4. Bake for 10 minutes, stir the nuts around, and bake another 5 minutes. Let cool on the foil and then store in a tin with a tight-fitting lid.

Serves 4

1 tablespoon heavy cream
1 tablespoon dark rum
¼ teaspoon Tabasco sauce
1 cup pecan halves
¼ cup brown sugar

🌶 RUM AND SUGAR

Most anywhere sugar cane grows rum is made, because rum is made from sugar cane. This includes the Caribbean. Jamaican rum is dark and slightly sweet, and Puerto Rican rum is lighter and drier. Whether the rum is dark, gold, white, or spiced, it is usually 80 proof, which means it is 40 percent alcohol. The exception is 151 rum, which is 75.5 percent alcohol. Beware!

Spicy Banana Pops

An easy, mix-and-freeze dessert that spices up a classic combo of bananas and chocolate. Add as much or as little cayenne as you like.

Yields 18 pops

4 cups milk

2 (3-ounce) packages instant vanilla pudding mix

3 bananas

1 tablespoon lime juice

¼ teaspoon ground ancho chili powder

⅛ teaspoon cayenne pepper

1 cup whipped cream

2 cups mini semisweet chocolate chips

18 paper drink cups

18 frozen-dessert sticks

1. In large bowl, combine milk and pudding mixes and beat with wire whisk until thickened.

2. In small bowl, mash bananas with lime juice and stir into pudding mixture.

3. Add chili powder and cayenne pepper, and fold in whipped cream and mini chocolate chips.

4. Divide mixture evenly among paper drink cups.

5. Place drink cups on baking sheet and freeze for 1–2 hours until just firm. Insert frozen-dessert sticks into banana mixture, return to freezer, and freeze for 3–4 hours until frozen solid. Peel away drink cups to serve.

Spiced Chocolate Cake

Serve this spicy, pressure cooker chocolate cake with icing, powdered sugar, or ice cream on top.

1. In a medium bowl, mix the flour, cocoa powder, cinnamon, cayenne, sugar, salt, and baking powder. In a large bowl, beat the eggs, if using. Add the dry ingredients to the eggs or bananas. Slowly stir in the melted butter or margarine and the milk or soymilk. Pour the cake mixture into an 8" round pan.

2. Add the steaming rack to the pressure cooker and pour in the hot water. Place the cake in the pressure cooker and lock the lid into place. Bring to high pressure, then reduce to low and cook for 30 minutes.

3. Remove the pressure cooker from the heat, quick-release the steam, and carefully remove the cake.

Serves 10–12

1½ cups all-purpose flour
4 tablespoons cocoa powder
1 teaspoon cinnamon
1 teaspoon cayenne pepper
1 teaspoon sugar
¼ teaspoon salt
1 teaspoon baking powder
2 eggs, beaten, or 2 mashed bananas
4 tablespoons butter or vegan margarine, such as Earth Balance, melted
1 cup milk or soymilk
2 cups hot water

Spiced Peaches

Spicy and simple to make, these pressure cooker Spiced Peaches will bring a smile to any face.

Serves 6

2 (15-ounce) cans sliced
   peaches in syrup
¼ cup water
1 tablespoon white wine vinegar
⅛ teaspoon ground allspice
1 cinnamon stick
4 whole cloves
½ teaspoon ground ginger
Pinch cayenne pepper
1 tablespoon candied ginger,
   minced
3 whole black peppercorns

1. Add all of the ingredients to the pressure cooker. Stir to mix. Lock the lid into place and bring to low pressure; maintain pressure for 3 minutes. Remove the pressure cooker from the heat, quick-release the pressure, and remove the lid. Remove and discard the cinnamon stick, cloves, and peppercorns.

2. Return to low heat. Simmer and stir for 5 minutes to thicken the syrup. Serve warm or chilled. To store, allow to cool and then refrigerate for up to a week.

🌶 MAKE SPICED PEACH BUTTER

To make spiced peach butter, after Step 2 process the peaches and liquid in a blender or food processor until smooth, and return to the pressure cooker. Simmer and stir over low heat for 30 minutes or until thickened enough to coat the back of a spoon.

Bloody Mary Mix

Instead of having to make the same drink over and over again, make a batch of this Bloody Mary Mix before having people over for brunch.

Mix all ingredients and refrigerate. You can add many types of ingredients to a basic Bloody Mary Mix: raw horseradish, lime juice, A1 Steak Sauce, wasabi, chili powder, bitters, or anything else you like. Go wild. Combine 2 cups Bloody Mary Mix with 1–2 shots of vodka to make a Bloody Mary.

Yields enough for 8 Bloody Marys

2 (46-ounce) cans tomato juice
Juice of 2 fresh lemons
2 tablespoons vegan Worcestershire sauce
1 tablespoon horseradish
¼ teaspoon cayenne pepper
½ teaspoon celery salt
½ teaspoon ground black pepper
Tabasco (or any hot sauce of your liking), to taste

Bloody Maria

The Bloody Mary goes south of the border with tequila and lime instead of vodka and a celery stalk.

Serves 1

2 lime wedges

¼ teaspoon celery salt

¼ teaspoon vegan Worcestershire sauce

⅛ teaspoon pepper

1 dash of Tabasco sauce

1 ounce tequila

5 ounces tomato juice

1. Run a lime wedge around the rim of a tall glass, then dip the rim in celery salt.

2. Fill the glass with ice and squeeze the same lime wedge into it.

3. Shake the celery salt, Worcestershire sauce, pepper, and Tabasco sauce into the glass.

4. Add the tequila and tomato juice and stir well with a long iced tea or bar spoon. Garnish with a lime wedge.

Micheladas

You can vary the ingredients in this classic Mexican drink to your taste. Try it with different kinds of beer too; dark ale will make a more robust Michelada than a light beer.

In a cocktail shaker, combine all ingredients except ice and shake to blend well. Strain over ice.

Serves 2

1 (16-ounce) bottle beer
2 tablespoons lime juice
¼ teaspoon Tabasco sauce
2 teaspoons vegan Worcestershire sauce
1 tablespoon soy sauce
½ teaspoon salt
2 cups crushed ice

🌶 IN THE LIQUOR STORE

In some liquor stores or grocery stores, you may be able to find a Michelada mix to add to cold beer. But the real fun lies in experimenting and adjusting the spices to your liking.

Cucumber Margaritas

Cucumbers offer a mild and cooling contrast in these pretty, light green drinks.

Serves 6

2 cucumbers
⅓ cup lime juice
2 tablespoons superfine sugar
½ cup tequila
½ teaspoon salt
¼ teaspoon cayenne pepper
1 cup crushed ice

1. Peel cucumber, cut in half, and remove seeds with a spoon. Cut into chunks and place in blender container or food processor with remaining ingredients. Cover and blend or process until mixture is smooth and thick.

2. Serve immediately, garnished with cucumber slices.

Hot-Blooded

Be very careful when lighting this on fire. It's all fun until somebody gets their face burned.

Pour the tequila into a shot glass and add several dashes of Tabasco. Gently layer the 151 rum on top, then light. Allow the flame to die out, then drink.

Yields 1 shot

1½ ounces tequila
Several dashes Tabasco
⅛ ounce 151 rum

🔥 FLAMING SHOTS

There is a common misconception that lighting a shot on fire concentrates the liquor and makes the drink stronger. In reality, lighting the liquor on fire makes the drink less strong. The fire burns away the alcohol and weakens the drink.

Prairie Fire Shooter

One taste and you'll understand why they call it fire. You can chase the shooter with a beer to calm the fire.

Yields 1 shot

1½ ounces tequila
3 dashes Tabasco

Pour tequila into a shot glass and add the Tabasco.

🔥 TEQUILA

Tequila is made from the blue agave, a cactus-like plant that grows in the area near the city of Tequila. True tequila must have a blue agave content of 51 percent, otherwise it is called mescal. Fine tequilas are 100 percent blue agave.

Metric Conversion Chart

VOLUME CONVERSIONS	
U.S. Volume Measure	**Metric Equivalent**
⅛ teaspoon	0.5 milliliter
¼ teaspoon	1 milliliter
½ teaspoon	2 milliliters
1 teaspoon	5 milliliters
½ tablespoon	7 milliliters
1 tablespoon (3 teaspoons)	15 milliliters
2 tablespoons (1 fluid ounce)	30 milliliters
¼ cup (4 tablespoons)	60 milliliters
⅓ cup	90 milliliters
½ cup (4 fluid ounces)	125 milliliters
⅔ cup	160 milliliters
¾ cup (6 fluid ounces)	180 milliliters
1 cup (16 tablespoons)	250 milliliters
1 pint (2 cups)	500 milliliters
1 quart (4 cups)	1 liter (about)
WEIGHT CONVERSIONS	
U.S. Weight Measure	**Metric Equivalent**
½ ounce	15 grams
1 ounce	30 grams
2 ounces	60 grams
3 ounces	85 grams
¼ pound (4 ounces)	115 grams
½ pound (8 ounces)	225 grams
¾ pound (12 ounces)	340 grams
1 pound (16 ounces)	454 grams

OVEN TEMPERATURE CONVERSIONS

Degrees Fahrenheit	Degrees Celsius
200 degrees F	95 degrees C
250 degrees F	120 degrees C
275 degrees F	135 degrees C
300 degrees F	150 degrees C
325 degrees F	160 degrees C
350 degrees F	180 degrees C
375 degrees F	190 degrees C
400 degrees F	205 degrees C
425 degrees F	220 degrees C
450 degrees F	230 degrees C

BAKING PAN SIZES

U.S.	Metric
8 x 1½ inch round baking pan	20 x 4 cm cake tin
9 x 1½ inch round baking pan	23 x 3.5 cm cake tin
11 x 7 x 1½ inch baking pan	28 x 18 x 4 cm baking tin
13 x 9 x 2 inch baking pan	30 x 20 x 5 cm baking tin
2 quart rectangular baking dish	30 x 20 x 3 cm baking tin
15 x 10 x 2 inch baking pan	30 x 25 x 2 cm baking tin (Swiss roll tin)
9 inch pie plate	22 x 4 or 23 x 4 cm pie plate
7 or 8 inch springform pan	18 or 20 cm springform or loose bottom cake tin
9 x 5 x 3 inch loaf pan	23 x 13 x 7 cm or 2 lb narrow loaf or pâté tin
1½ quart casserole	1.5 liter casserole
2 quart casserole	2 liter casserole

Pepper Identification Charts

Capsicum frutescens			
Name	Color	Heat Level (Scoville Heat Units)	Average Size
Tabasco	light yellow, ripens red	30,000–50,000 SHU	1–1.5" long, 1" wide
Thai Bird's Eye	green, ripens to red	50,000–100,000 SHU	1" long, .5" wide
Piri Piri	green, ripens to purple or red	50,000–175,000 SHU	4" long, 1" wide
Malagueta	green, ripens to red	60,000–100,000 SHU	2" long, .5" wide
Japone	red	20,000–25,000 SHU	1–3.5" long, .5" wide
Bangalore Torpedo	lime green, ripens to red	16,000–50,000 SHU	5" long, .5" wide
Dagger Pod	green, ripens through orange to red	30,000–50,000 SHU	4" long, .5" wide
Kambuzi/ Malawian	yellow, orange, red	50,000–175,000 SHU	1–1.5" long, 1.5" wide

Capsicum annuum			
Name	Color	Heat Level (Scoville Heat Units)	Average Size
Jalapeño	green, ripens to red	2,000–5,000 SHU	2.5–3" long, 1–1.5" wide
Poblano	dark, deep green	1,000–2,000 SHU	4.5" long, 1.5–2" wide
Anaheim	light green	500–2,500 SHU	6–7" long, 1.5–2" wide
New Mexico	dark green, ripens to bright red	1,000–1,500 SHU	4–6" long, 1–1.5" wide
Serrano	green, ripens to red	8,000–22,000 SHU	3" long, .5" wide
New Mexico Big Jim	green, ripens to red	500–1,000 SHU	8–10" long, 2.5–3" wide
Casabella	yellow, red	1,500–4,000 SHU	1.5" long, .5" wide
Bola	red	1,000–2,500 SHU	1.5" long, 1.5" wide
Cayenne	red	30,000–50,000 SHU	4" long, .5–1" wide
Charleston Hot	green, ripens to bright orange	80,000–100,000 SHU	3" long, .5" wide
Cherry Bomb	green, ripens to bright red	2,500–5,000 SHU	2" long, 3" wide
De Árbol	red	15,000–30,000 SHU	3" long, .5" wide
Fresno	green, ripens to bright red	3,000–8,000 SHU	3" long, 1" wide
Goat Horn	green, ripens to bright red	5,000–8,000 SHU	5–6" long, 1" wide
Hungarian Yellow Wax	yellow, ripens to orange-red	2,000–4,000 SHU	5" long, 1" wide
Pepperoncini	green, ripens to red	100–500 SHU	3.5" long, 1" wide
Piquin	red	30,000–40,000 SHU	1" long, .5" wide

Capsicum annuum

Name	Color	Heat Level (Scoville Heat Units)	Average Size
Padron	green	1000–1,500 SHU	4" long, 1–1.5" wide
Shishito	green, ripens to red	1,000–2,000 SHU	3.5" long, .5–1" wide
Thai Dragon	green, ripens to red	75,000–100,000 SHU	2–3" long, .5" wide

Capsicum pubescens

Name	Color	Heat Level (Scoville Heat Units)	Average Size
Rocoto	green, ripens to red	225,000–350,000 SHU	2–3" long, 1" wide
Manzano	green, ripening to yellow, orange, and red	12,000–30,000 SHU	1.5–2" long, .5–1" wide

Capsicum baccatum

Name	Color	Heat Level (Scoville Heat Units)	Average Size
Aji	yellow, ripens to orange	40,000–50,000 SHU	4" long, 1" wide
Aji Cereza	bright red	70,000–80,000 SHU	1" long, 1" wide
Peppadew	green, ripens to bright red	1,000–5,000 SHU	1" long, 1" wide
Brazilian Starfish	red	5,000–20,000 SHU	1" long, 2" wide
Christmas Bell	red	100–500 SHU	2" long, 1.5" wide

Capsicum chinense			
Name	Color	Heat Level (Scoville Heat Units)	Average Size
Habanero	green, ripens to orange or red	200,000–300,000 SHU	1–1.5" long, 1–1.5" wide
Scotch Bonnet	green, ripens to bright orange and red	100,000–350,000 SHU	1–1.5" long, 1–1.5" wide
Naga Jolokia (Ghost Pepper)	green, ripens to deep red	800,000–1,000,000 SHU	2.5–3" long, 1–1.5" wide
Madame Jeanette	yellow, bright red	175,000–225,000 SHU	2.5" long, 1–1.5" wide
Hainan Yellow Lantern	yellow	175,000–350,000 SHU	2" long, 1" wide
Aji Dulce	green, ripens to red	200,000–350,000 SHU	1" long, 2" wide
Facing Heaven	bright red	200,000–500,000 SHU	2.5" long, 1.5" wide
Datil	dark yellow and orange	200,000–300,000 SHU	3" long, .5" wide
Habanero Red Savina	red	350,000–575,000 SHU	2" long, 1.5" wide
Jamaican Hot Chocolate	chocolate brown when ripe	100,000–200,000 SHU	2.5" long, 1.5" wide
Paper Lantern Habanero	lime green, orange, bright red	300,000–500,000 SHU	2" long, .5–1" wide
Aji Limo	yellow, ripens through purple and orange to red	50,000–60,000 SHU	2" long, 1.5" wide

INDEX